Introduction to Arduino Nano

Overview of Arduino Nano

The **Arduino Nano** is a small but powerful microcontroller board designed for electronics projects. It is a compact version of the popular **Arduino Uno**, making it ideal for projects where space is limited.

What Makes Arduino Nano Special?

- **Size:** It is **tiny** (only about 45mm long and 18mm wide), making it perfect for small devices and wearable projects.

- **USB Connectivity:** It has a **mini-USB** or **Type-C** port for easy programming and power supply.

- **Microcontroller:** It uses the **ATmega328P** chip, the same as the Arduino Uno, so most programs written for Uno will work on Nano.

- **Pins:** It has **30 pins**, including **digital inputs/outputs, analog inputs, and power pins**. These allow you to connect buttons, sensors, LEDs, motors, and more.

- **Built-in LED:** There is a small LED on pin 13 that can be used for quick testing.

What Can You Do with Arduino Nano?

- Control LEDs, motors, and sensors.

- Read data from temperature, light, or motion sensors.

- Build small robots, smart devices, and automation systems.

- Send and receive data using Bluetooth or WiFi (with additional modules).

The **Arduino Nano** is a great choice for beginners and advanced users alike. It is easy to program, has many features, and can be used in **hundreds of exciting projects**.

Key features and specifications

The **Arduino Nano** is a small but powerful microcontroller board. It has everything needed to control electronic components like LEDs, motors, and sensors. Here are its key features and specifications:

1. Small Size, Big Power

- The **Arduino Nano** is tiny (**45mm x 18mm**) but just as powerful as the larger **Arduino Uno**.

- It fits easily into small projects, making it perfect for **wearable tech, compact gadgets, and DIY electronics**.

2. ATmega328P Microcontroller

- The Nano runs on an **ATmega328P** chip, the same one used in the Arduino Uno.

- It can store and run programs written in **C/C++** using the **Arduino IDE**.

3. Input and Output Pins

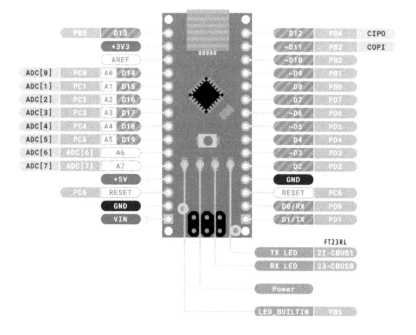

Arduino Nano - Basics of Proper Programming

Source https://docs.arduino.cc/resources/pinouts/A000005-full-pinout.pdf,
Access: 2005.02.14

Legend:

Ground   Digital Pin

Power   Analog Pin

LED   Other Pin

Internal Pin   Microcontroller's Port

SWD Pin   Default

Note:

MAXIMUM current per I/O pin is 20mA.

MAXIMUM current per +3.3V pin is 50mA

IN 7-12 V input to the board.

CIPO/COPI have previously been referred to as MISO/MOSI

- **14 digital pins** – Used for reading button presses, controlling LEDs, motors, and more.

- **6 analog pins** – Can read signals from sensors like temperature and light sensors.

- **PWM support** – Some digital pins can produce Pulse Width Modulation (PWM) signals to control motors and LED brightness.

4. USB Connectivity

- The Nano has a **mini-USB** or **Type-C** port (depending on the version).

- This allows easy connection to a computer for programming and power.

5. Memory and Speed

- **Flash Memory:** 32 KB (where your program is stored).

- **RAM (SRAM):** 2 KB (for temporary data while the program runs).

- **EEPROM:** 1 KB (for storing small amounts of data that stay even when the power is off).

- **Clock Speed:** 16 MHz (fast enough for most embedded applications).

6. Power Options

- Can be powered through **USB (5V)** or an **external power source (7-12V)**.

- Has a **voltage regulator** that converts higher voltage to a safe 5V for the microcontroller.

7. Built-in LED for Quick Testing

- The Nano has a small **LED connected to Pin 13**, which can be used for simple tests (like blinking).

The **Arduino Nano** is compact, reliable, and easy to use, making it an excellent choice for beginners and experienced makers alike.

Setting up your development environment

Before you can start programming your **Arduino Nano**, you need to set up your development environment. This involves installing software, connecting the board, and testing everything to make sure it works. Follow these simple steps to get started.

1. Install the Arduino IDE

The **Arduino IDE (Integrated Development Environment)** is the software used to write and upload code to your Arduino Nano.

Steps to Install the Arduino IDE:

1. Go to the official **Arduino website**: https://www.arduino.cc/en/software.

2. Download the version for your operating system (**Windows, macOS, or Linux**).

3. Run the installer and follow the on-screen instructions.

Once installed, open the Arduino IDE to check if it's working.

2. Connect the Arduino Nano to Your Computer

The **Arduino Nano** is programmed through a **USB cable**. Some Nano models use a **Mini-USB cable**, while newer versions use **USB Type-C**.

Steps to Connect:

1. Plug the USB cable into the **Arduino Nano**.

2. Connect the other end to your **computer's USB port**.

3. If this is your first time, wait for your computer to **install drivers automatically**.

If the drivers don't install automatically, you may need to install them manually (especially for **clone versions** of the Nano that use the CH340 chip).

3. Select the Correct Board and Port

To program the Nano, the Arduino IDE needs to know which board you are using and which port it is connected to.

Steps to Select the Board:

1. Open the **Arduino IDE**.

2. Go to **Tools → Board → Arduino Nano**.

Steps to Select the Port:

1. Go to **Tools → Port**.

2. Select the **COM port** that appears (it usually looks like "COM3" or "COM4" on Windows or "/dev/ttyUSB0" on macOS/Linux).

4. Install the Right Bootloader (If Needed)

Some versions of the **Arduino Nano** use the **Old Bootloader**. If your Nano doesn't work right away, try switching the bootloader:

1. Go to **Tools → Processor**.

2. Select **ATmega328P (Old Bootloader)**.

5. Test with a Simple Program

To check if your setup is correct, upload a simple **Blink program** that makes the built-in LED turn on and off.

Steps to Upload the Blink Program:

1. In the **Arduino IDE**, go to **File → Examples → Basics → Blink**.

2. Click the **Upload** button (a right-facing arrow).

3. Wait for the upload to finish. If everything is working, the small LED on your Nano should start blinking.

Now You're Ready to Code!

You've successfully set up your **Arduino Nano**! Now you can start writing your own programs and experimenting with sensors, motors, and other components.

Getting Started with C/C++ for Arduino

Basics of C/C++ programming

The **Arduino Nano** is programmed using **C/C++**, a powerful and widely used programming language. Don't worry if you've never used C/C++ before! You only need to understand a few basic concepts to start writing Arduino programs (called **sketches**).

1. Structure of an Arduino Program

Every Arduino program has **two main parts**:

```
void setup() {
  // Code inside setup runs once when the Arduino is powered on
}


void loop() {
  // Code inside loop runs over and over again
}
```

- **setup()** – Runs **once** at the beginning. Used to set up pins, sensors, and communication.

- **loop()** – Runs **continuously** after setup(). This is where your main program logic goes.

2. Writing and Displaying Text

Arduino can send messages to your computer using the **Serial Monitor**.

```
void setup() {
  Serial.begin(9600);  // Start communication at 9600 baud
  Serial.println("Hello, Arduino!");  // Print text to Serial Monitor
```

```
}


void loop() {

  // Nothing here for now

}
```

- **Serial.begin(9600);** – Starts communication at **9600 baud** (standard speed).

- **Serial.println("Hello, Arduino!");** – Prints text on the Serial Monitor.

3. Variables and Data Types

A **variable** stores a value that your program can use.

```
int number = 10;    // Integer variable

float pi = 3.14;    // Decimal number

char letter = 'A';  // Single character

bool isOn = true;   // Boolean (true/false)
```

Common data types in Arduino:

- **int** – Whole numbers (**-32,768 to 32,767**)

- **float** – Decimal numbers (**3.14, -0.5, 2.71**)

- **char** – Single characters (**'A', 'B', 'C'**)

- **bool** – true or false

4. Operators

Operators are used for calculations and comparisons.

```
int a = 5;

int b = 2;

int sum = a + b;   // Addition (7)

int diff = a - b; // Subtraction (3)

int product = a * b;  // Multiplication (10)
```

```
int division = a / b; // Division (2, because both are
integers)
```

Comparison operators:

- == (equal to)

- != (not equal to)

- > (greater than)

- < (less than)

Example:

```
if (a > b) {
  Serial.println("a is greater than b");
}
```

5. If Statements (Decision Making)

if statements let you run code only when a condition is met.

```
int temperature = 25;


if (temperature > 30) {
  Serial.println("It's hot!");
} else {
  Serial.println("It's not too hot.");
}
```

6. Loops (Repeating Code)

Loops **repeat** actions multiple times.

For Loop (Counted Repeats)

```
for (int i = 0; i < 5; i++) {
  Serial.println("Counting: " + String(i));
}
```

While Loop (Repeats Until Condition is False)

```
int count = 0;
while (count < 5) {
  Serial.println(count);
  count++;  // Increase count by 1 each time
}
```

7. Functions (Reusable Code Blocks)

Functions let you **organize your code** into smaller, reusable parts.

```
void sayHello() {
  Serial.println("Hello, World!");
}


void loop() {
  sayHello();  // Call the function
  delay(1000); // Wait 1 second
}
```

8. Controlling Digital Outputs (Example: LED Blinking)

```
void setup() {
  pinMode(13, OUTPUT);  // Set pin 13 as output
}


void loop() {
  digitalWrite(13, HIGH); // Turn LED on
  delay(1000);            // Wait 1 second
  digitalWrite(13, LOW);  // Turn LED off
  delay(1000);            // Wait 1 second
```

}

Now You Know the Basics!

These are the **fundamental concepts** of C/C++ for Arduino. With this knowledge, you can start writing your own Arduino programs and control sensors, motors, and displays!

Understanding the Arduino IDE

The **Arduino IDE (Integrated Development Environment)** is the software used to write, edit, and upload code to your **Arduino Nano**. It is simple to use and has all the tools needed to program your board.

1. Download and Install the Arduino IDE

To start using the **Arduino IDE**, you need to install it on your computer.

Steps to Install:

1. Go to the official Arduino website: https://www.arduino.cc/en/software.

2. Download the version for your operating system (**Windows, macOS, or Linux**).

3. Run the installer and follow the on-screen instructions.

4. Open the **Arduino IDE** after installation.

2. Exploring the Arduino IDE Interface

When you open the Arduino IDE, you will see several important sections:

◆ **Menu Bar** – Provides options for file management, editing, and tools.
◆ **Toolbar** – Buttons for verifying, uploading, and opening sketches.
◆ **Sketch Area** – This is where you write and edit your code.
◆ **Message Area** – Displays errors and status messages.
◆ **Serial Monitor** – Allows communication with the Arduino board.

3. Writing and Saving a Program (Sketch)

A program in the Arduino IDE is called a **sketch**.

Steps to Create a New Sketch:

1. Click **File → New** to open a blank sketch.

2. Write your code in the **sketch area**.

3. Click **File → Save** to store your work.

Example Sketch (Blinking LED):

```
void setup() {

  pinMode(13, OUTPUT); // Set pin 13 as an output

}


void loop() {

  digitalWrite(13, HIGH); // Turn LED on

  delay(1000); // Wait 1 second

  digitalWrite(13, LOW); // Turn LED off

  delay(1000); // Wait 1 second

}
```

4. Selecting the Correct Board and Port

Before uploading code, you need to tell the IDE which Arduino board you are using.

Steps to Select the Board:

1. Go to **Tools → Board**.

2. Select **Arduino Nano** from the list.

Steps to Select the Port:

1. Go to **Tools → Port**.

2. Choose the port where your **Arduino Nano** is connected (e.g., **COM3** on Windows or **/dev/ttyUSB0** on macOS/Linux).

5. Uploading a Sketch to the Arduino Nano

Once your board and port are selected, you can upload your program.

Steps to Upload a Sketch:

1. Click the **Checkmark (✓☐) button** to verify your code for errors.

2. Click the **Arrow (→☐) button** to upload the sketch to the Arduino Nano.

3. Wait for the message **"Done Uploading"** in the status bar.

If everything is working, the built-in LED on **Pin 13** should start blinking!

6. Using the Serial Monitor

The **Serial Monitor** allows you to communicate with your Arduino and display messages from your program.

Steps to Open the Serial Monitor:

1. Click **Tools → Serial Monitor**.

2. Set the baud rate to **9600** (or match the value in Serial.begin() in your sketch).

Example Code to Print Messages:

```
void setup() {

  Serial.begin(9600);

  Serial.println("Hello, Arduino!");

}


void loop() {

  Serial.println("This message repeats!");

  delay(1000);

}
```

When you open the **Serial Monitor**, you will see messages appearing every second!

Now You Know the Arduino IDE!

With the **Arduino IDE**, you can write, test, and upload code to your Arduino Nano. Now you're ready to start creating projects!

Writing your first program

Now that you have set up your **Arduino Nano** and understand the **Arduino IDE**, it's time to write your first program! In this section, you will learn how to create a simple program (called a **sketch**) that makes an LED blink.

1. Understanding the Blink Program

Your first program will turn the built-in LED **on and off** repeatedly. This is a great way to test if your Arduino Nano is working correctly.

What You Will Learn:

✓ How to control an output pin
✓ How to use delays in a program
✓ How to upload and run a sketch

2. Writing the Blink Program

Step 1: Open the Arduino IDE

1. Launch the **Arduino IDE** on your computer.

2. Click **File → New** to create a new sketch.

Step 2: Type the Following Code

```
void setup() {
  pinMode(13, OUTPUT);  // Set pin 13 as an output
}


void loop() {
  digitalWrite(13, HIGH); // Turn LED on
  delay(1000);            // Wait for 1 second
  digitalWrite(13, LOW);  // Turn LED off
  delay(1000);            // Wait for 1 second
}
```

Step 3: Save Your Sketch

1. Click **File → Save As** and give your program a name (e.g., BlinkTest).

2. Click **Save**.

3. Understanding the Code

✓ void setup()

- Runs **once** when the Arduino is powered on.

- pinMode(13, OUTPUT); → Sets **pin 13** as an output to control the LED.

✓ void loop()

- Runs **repeatedly** after setup().

- digitalWrite(13, HIGH); → Turns the LED **on**.

- delay(1000); → Waits **1000 milliseconds (1 second)**.

- digitalWrite(13, LOW); → Turns the LED **off**.

- delay(1000); → Waits **another second** before repeating.

4. Uploading the Program to Arduino Nano

Step 1: Connect the Arduino Nano

1. Plug your **Arduino Nano** into your computer using a USB cable.

2. Make sure the correct **board and port** are selected in the **Arduino IDE**:

   ○ Go to **Tools → Board → Arduino Nano**.

   ○ Go to **Tools → Port** and select the correct port.

Step 2: Upload the Program

1. Click the **Checkmark (✓☐) button** to verify your code.

2. Click the **Upload (➡☐) button** to send the code to your Arduino Nano.

3. Wait for the message **"Done Uploading"** in the status bar.

5. Watch the LED Blink!

If everything is set up correctly, the small **LED on your Arduino Nano (Pin 13)** should start blinking **on and off every second!** 🖌️

◆ **LED ON → Wait 1 second → LED OFF → Wait 1 second → Repeat**

Now You're Ready to Experiment!

Congratulations! 🖌️ You have successfully written and uploaded your **first Arduino program**. Now, try modifying the **delay times** to make the LED blink faster or slower! 🚀

Example: Change delay(1000); to delay(500); and see what happens!

Understanding Arduino Sketches

Structure of an Arduino sketch

An **Arduino sketch** is a simple program written in **C/C++** that tells the **Arduino Nano** what to do. Every sketch follows the same basic structure, making it easy to read and understand.

1. The Two Main Parts of a Sketch

Every Arduino program has **two required functions**:

```
void setup() {

  // Code here runs once when the Arduino starts

}


void loop() {

  // Code here runs repeatedly

}
```

✓ **setup()** → Runs **once** at the beginning. It is used to initialize pins, sensors, and communication.

✓ **loop()** → Runs **over and over** after setup(). This is where the main code goes.

2. Example: Basic LED Blink Sketch

```
void setup() {

  pinMode(13, OUTPUT);  // Set pin 13 as an output

}


void loop() {

  digitalWrite(13, HIGH); // Turn LED on

  delay(1000);            // Wait 1 second

  digitalWrite(13, LOW);  // Turn LED off
```

```
   delay(1000);                // Wait 1 second
}
```

✓ **pinMode(13, OUTPUT);** – Tells the Arduino that **pin 13** will be used as an **output**.

✓ **digitalWrite(13, HIGH);** – Turns the LED **on**.

✓ **delay(1000);** – Waits **1 second**.

✓ **digitalWrite(13, LOW);** – Turns the LED **off**.

✓ **delay(1000);** – Waits **another second** before repeating.

3. Additional Optional Parts of a Sketch

While only setup() and loop() are required, you can add **other sections** to make your code more organized.

(A) Comments – Notes for Humans

Comments help explain what the code does. They **don't affect** how the program runs.

- **Single-line comment** (starts with //):

```
// This is a comment
```

- **Multi-line comment** (starts with /* and ends with */):

```
/*
   This is a multi-line comment.
   It can span multiple lines.
*/
```

(B) Variables – Storing Data

Variables store values like numbers, text, or sensor readings.

```
int ledPin = 13; // Store pin number in a variable
```

(C) Custom Functions – Organizing Code

Functions allow you to **break your code into smaller parts** to make it easier to manage.

```
void blinkLED() {
```

```
digitalWrite(13, HIGH);

delay(1000);

digitalWrite(13, LOW);

delay(1000);
}
```

4. Summary: The Basic Structure of an Arduino Sketch

✓ **setup()** – Runs **once** at the beginning to set things up.
✓ **loop()** – Runs **forever**, executing the main program repeatedly.
✓ **Optional:**

- **Comments** (// or /* */) help explain the code.

- **Variables** store data for use in the program.

- **Custom functions** make the code more organized.

With this structure, you can **write, understand, and modify** Arduino programs easily! 🚀

Setup and loop functions explained

Every **Arduino sketch** (program) has two essential functions:

- **setup()** → Runs **once** when the Arduino is powered on.

- **loop()** → Runs **continuously**, repeating the main program.

These functions **control how your Arduino works**, so understanding them is key to writing good programs.

1. The setup() Function – Initialization

The **setup() function** is used to **prepare** the Arduino before the main program starts running.

When Does setup() Run?

✓ It runs **only once**, right after the Arduino is powered on or reset.
✓ It is used to **configure settings** like pin modes, serial communication, and sensors.

Example of setup() Function:

```
void setup() {

  pinMode(13, OUTPUT);   // Set pin 13 as an output

  Serial.begin(9600);    // Start serial communication at
9600 baud

}
```

✓ **pinMode(13, OUTPUT);** → Configures **pin 13** as an output to control an LED.
✓ **Serial.begin(9600);** → Starts **serial communication** to send messages to the computer.

2. The loop() Function – Main Program Execution

After setup() finishes, the **loop() function** starts running.

When Does loop() Run?

✓ It runs **forever**, repeating the code inside it over and over.
✓ It is where you place the **main logic** of your program, such as reading sensors or controlling LEDs.

Example of loop() Function:

```
void loop() {

  digitalWrite(13, HIGH); // Turn LED on

  delay(1000);            // Wait 1 second

  digitalWrite(13, LOW);  // Turn LED off

  delay(1000);            // Wait 1 second

}
```

✓ The LED **turns on** → waits 1 second → **turns off** → waits 1 second → **repeats forever**.

3. How setup() and loop() Work Together

When an **Arduino starts**, the sequence is:

1. The setup() function runs **once** (to set up pins, communication, etc.).
2. The loop() function starts and **keeps running forever**, executing the main program.

Complete Example:

```
void setup() {

  Serial.begin(9600);  // Initialize serial communication

}


void loop() {

  Serial.println("Hello, Arduino!");  // Print a message

  delay(1000);  // Wait 1 second

}
```

◆ setup() runs once to start the **Serial Monitor**.
◆ loop() **keeps printing** "Hello, Arduino!" every second.

4. Summary: Why setup() and loop() Matter

✓ **setup()** → Runs **once** to configure settings.
✓ **loop()** → Runs **forever**, repeating the main program.
✓ Together, they **ensure the Arduino works properly** for any task, whether it's controlling LEDs, reading sensors, or sending data.

Now that you understand setup() and loop(), you are ready to start building **your own Arduino programs!**

Uploading sketches to the Arduino Nano

Once you've written your **Arduino sketch**, you need to upload it to your **Arduino Nano** so it can start running the program. Follow these simple steps to upload your code successfully.

1. Connect the Arduino Nano to Your Computer

To upload a sketch, first, you need to connect your **Arduino Nano** to your computer using a **USB cable**.

Steps to Connect:

1. Plug one end of the **USB cable** into the Arduino Nano.

2. Connect the other end to your **computer's USB port**.

3. If it's your first time using the Nano, wait for the drivers to install automatically.

◆ If your computer does not recognize the board, you may need to install the **CH340 driver** (used by some clone versions of the Nano).

2. Open the Arduino IDE and Select the Correct Board

Now, open the **Arduino IDE** and tell it which board you're using.

Steps to Select the Board:

1. Open the **Arduino IDE**.

2. Go to **Tools → Board** and select **Arduino Nano**.

3. Go to **Tools → Processor** and choose **ATmega328P (Old Bootloader)** if your Nano doesn't work with the default option.

3. Select the Correct Port

The **port** is the connection between your Arduino and your computer.

Steps to Select the Port:

1. Go to **Tools → Port**.

2. Select the port where your **Arduino Nano** is connected. (It usually looks like **COM3, COM4, etc.** on Windows or **/dev/ttyUSB0** on macOS/Linux.)

◆ If no port appears, try unplugging and reconnecting the USB cable.

4. Upload Your Sketch

Now you're ready to **upload** your code to the Arduino Nano!

Steps to Upload a Sketch:

1. Click the **Checkmark (✓□) button** to verify your code for errors.

2. Click the **Upload (➡□) button** to send the code to your Arduino.

3. Wait for the message **"Done Uploading"** in the status bar.

5. Verify the Upload

If the upload is successful:

✓ The **LED on the Nano will blink quickly** during the upload.

✓ The message **"Done Uploading"** appears in the Arduino IDE.

If the upload **fails**, try:

- Checking the **USB connection**.

- Selecting **ATmega328P (Old Bootloader)** under **Tools → Processor**.

- Choosing the correct **port**.

6. Test Your Uploaded Program

If you uploaded a **Blink** sketch, you should see the built-in LED **blinking** every second.

Example Blink Code to Test:

```
void setup() {

  pinMode(13, OUTPUT);

}


void loop() {

  digitalWrite(13, HIGH);

  delay(1000);

  digitalWrite(13, LOW);

  delay(1000);

}
```

If the LED **blinks**, your upload was successful! ✏️

Now You're Ready to Code!

You have successfully uploaded your first sketch to the **Arduino Nano**. Now, you can start experimenting with **sensors, motors, and other components** to build exciting projects!

Working with Digital I/O

Reading digital inputs

Digital inputs allow your **Arduino Nano** to read signals from external components, such as **buttons, switches, or sensors**. These inputs can be **ON (HIGH)** or **OFF (LOW)**, helping the Arduino detect simple conditions like a button press.

1. Understanding Digital Inputs

A **digital input** can have only two states:
✓ **HIGH (1)** – When the pin receives **5V** (ON).
✓ **LOW (0)** – When the pin receives **0V** (OFF).

For example, if you connect a **button** to a digital input pin, pressing the button might **send a HIGH signal**, while releasing it might **send a LOW signal**.

2. Setting Up a Digital Input in Arduino

To read a digital input, you need to:
1️⃣ **Choose a digital pin** (e.g., Pin 2).
2️⃣ **Set the pin as an INPUT** in setup().
3️⃣ **Read the pin's value** using digitalRead().

Example: Reading a Button Press

```
int buttonPin = 2;  // Button connected to digital pin 2

int buttonState;    // Variable to store button state


void setup() {

  pinMode(buttonPin, INPUT);  // Set pin 2 as an input

  Serial.begin(9600);         // Start Serial Monitor for
debugging

}


void loop() {
```

```
  buttonState = digitalRead(buttonPin);   // Read the
button state

  Serial.println(buttonState);             // Print the
state (0 or 1)

  delay(200);   // Short delay to avoid too many readings

}
```

✓ pinMode(buttonPin, INPUT); → Configures **Pin 2** as an **input**.
✓ digitalRead(buttonPin); → Reads **HIGH or LOW** from the button.
✓ Serial.println(buttonState); → Displays the button state in the **Serial Monitor**.

3. Using a Pull-Down Resistor for Reliable Input

When a button is **not pressed**, the input pin might be **floating** (not connected to HIGH or LOW), leading to **random readings**. To fix this, we use a **pull-down resistor** (10kΩ) to keep the input LOW until the button is pressed.

Wiring Diagram (Pull-Down Resistor Setup)

- **One side** of the button → **5V**

- **Other side** of the button → **Pin 2** and **10kΩ resistor**

- **Other side of the resistor** → **GND**

Alternatively, you can use **Arduino's built-in pull-up resistor** to avoid using an external resistor.

```
pinMode(buttonPin, INPUT_PULLUP);   // Enables internal
pull-up resistor
```

✓ This inverts the logic: **Pressed = LOW, Released = HIGH**.

---

4. Example: Turning an LED On/Off with a Button

```
int buttonPin = 2;

int ledPin = 13;

int buttonState;
```

```
void setup() {

  pinMode(buttonPin, INPUT_PULLUP);  // Internal pull-up
resistor enabled

  pinMode(ledPin, OUTPUT);

}


void loop() {

  buttonState = digitalRead(buttonPin);


  if (buttonState == LOW) {  // Button pressed

    digitalWrite(ledPin, HIGH);  // Turn LED on

  } else {  // Button released

    digitalWrite(ledPin, LOW);  // Turn LED off

  }

}
```

✓ When the button is pressed, the LED **turns on**.
✓ When the button is released, the LED **turns off**.

Now You Can Read Digital Inputs!

You've learned how to read signals from a **button** using digitalRead(). This same method works for **switches, motion sensors, and other digital input devices**. Try modifying the code to control motors or displays!

Controlling digital outputs

Digital outputs allow your **Arduino Nano** to control external components like **LEDs, buzzers, motors, and relays**. By setting a digital output pin to **HIGH (ON)** or **LOW (OFF)**, you can turn devices on and off easily.

1. Understanding Digital Outputs

A **digital output** has only two states:

✓ **HIGH (1, ON)** – Sends **5V** to the connected device.

✓ **LOW (0, OFF)** – Sends **0V** (ground).

For example, if you connect an **LED** to a digital output pin, setting the pin **HIGH** will turn the LED on, and setting it **LOW** will turn it off.

2. Setting Up a Digital Output in Arduino

To control a digital output, you need to:

1. **Choose a digital pin** (e.g., Pin 13).
2. **Set the pin as an OUTPUT** in setup().
3. **Use digitalWrite()** to turn it ON or OFF in loop().

Example: Turning an LED On and Off

```
int ledPin = 13;   // LED connected to digital pin 13


void setup() {

  pinMode(ledPin, OUTPUT);   // Set pin 13 as an output

}


void loop() {

  digitalWrite(ledPin, HIGH);   // Turn LED on

  delay(1000);                  // Wait 1 second

  digitalWrite(ledPin, LOW);    // Turn LED off

  delay(1000);                  // Wait 1 second

}
```

✓ pinMode(ledPin, OUTPUT); → Configures **Pin 13** as an **output**.

✓ digitalWrite(ledPin, HIGH); → Turns the LED **ON**.

✓ digitalWrite(ledPin, LOW); → Turns the LED **OFF**.

✓ delay(1000); → Adds a 1-second pause between state changes.

3. Using Digital Outputs with Other Devices

Digital outputs can control **many electronic components**, not just LEDs. Here are some examples:

✓ **Buzzer:**

```
int buzzer = 9;


void setup() {
  pinMode(buzzer, OUTPUT);
}


void loop() {
  digitalWrite(buzzer, HIGH);  // Turn buzzer ON
  delay(500);
  digitalWrite(buzzer, LOW);   // Turn buzzer OFF
  delay(500);
}
```

✓ Relay (to switch high-power devices like lamps):

```
int relay = 7;


void setup() {
  pinMode(relay, OUTPUT);
}


void loop() {
  digitalWrite(relay, HIGH);  // Turn relay ON
  delay(2000);
  digitalWrite(relay, LOW);   // Turn relay OFF
```

```
  delay(2000);
}
```

4. Summary: How to Control Digital Outputs

✓ **Digital outputs send either HIGH (ON) or LOW (OFF) signals.**
✓ **Use pinMode(pin, OUTPUT);** to set a pin as an output.
✓ **Use digitalWrite(pin, HIGH); and digitalWrite(pin, LOW); to control the output.**
✓ Digital outputs can control **LEDs, buzzers, motors, relays, and more**.

Now that you know how to control digital outputs, you can start building **exciting projects** like flashing LED patterns, sound alarms, or even smart home automation!

Practical projects: LED blinking, button press detection

Now that you understand **digital inputs and outputs**, let's apply them in simple, practical projects. We will create:

✓ **A blinking LED** – The basic starting point for any Arduino project.
✓ **A button-controlled LED** – A step towards interactive projects.

Project 1: Blinking an LED

This is the simplest Arduino project. The **LED will turn on and off every second**.

Wiring

- Connect an **LED** to **pin 13** (or use the built-in LED).

- Connect the **GND** pin to the **short leg** of the LED.

Code: Blinking LED

```
void setup() {
  pinMode(13, OUTPUT);   // Set pin 13 as an output
}
```

```
void loop() {

  digitalWrite(13, HIGH); // Turn LED on

  delay(1000);            // Wait 1 second

  digitalWrite(13, LOW);  // Turn LED off

  delay(1000);            // Wait 1 second

}
```

◆ **How It Works:**

✔ pinMode(13, OUTPUT); – Configures pin 13 as an output.

✔ digitalWrite(13, HIGH); – Turns the LED on.

✔ delay(1000); – Waits 1 second before switching states.

✔ digitalWrite(13, LOW); – Turns the LED off.

Project 2: LED Control with a Button

In this project, an LED will turn **ON when you press a button** and turn **OFF when you release it**.

Wiring

- Connect a **push button** to **pin 2**.

- Use an **internal pull-up resistor** (so we don't need an external resistor).

- Connect an **LED** to **pin 13**.

Code: LED Button Control

```
int buttonPin = 2;  // Button connected to pin 2

int ledPin = 13;    // LED connected to pin 13


void setup() {

  pinMode(buttonPin, INPUT_PULLUP); // Enable internal
pull-up resistor

  pinMode(ledPin, OUTPUT);

}
```

```
void loop() {

  int buttonState = digitalRead(buttonPin); // Read button
state

  if (buttonState == LOW) {  // Button pressed

    digitalWrite(ledPin, HIGH); // Turn LED on

  } else {  // Button released

    digitalWrite(ledPin, LOW);  // Turn LED off

  }

}
```

◆ **How It Works:**
✓ pinMode(buttonPin, INPUT_PULLUP); – Enables **internal pull-up resistor**, keeping the button HIGH by default.
✓ digitalRead(buttonPin); – Reads the button's state.
✓ If **button is pressed (LOW)** → LED **turns on**.
✓ If **button is released (HIGH)** → LED **turns off**.

Summary: What You Learned

✓ **Blinking LED** – A basic example of controlling digital outputs.
✓ **Button-controlled LED** – A simple interactive project using digital inputs.

These projects form the **foundation** of Arduino programming. Next, try expanding them by adding **buzzer sounds, multiple LEDs, or motor control!**

Analog I/O and Sensor Integration

Reading analog inputs

Unlike digital inputs, which can only detect **ON (HIGH)** or **OFF (LOW)** states, **analog inputs** can read a **range of values**. This is useful when working with **sensors** like temperature sensors, light sensors, and potentiometers.

1. What is an Analog Input?

An **analog input** allows the **Arduino Nano** to read **variable voltage levels** between **0V and 5V**. This is useful for measuring **light intensity, temperature, sound levels, and more**.

The Arduino Nano has **6 analog input pins (A0 to A5)**, which can read **values from 0 to 1023** using a built-in **10-bit analog-to-digital converter (ADC)**.

Voltage (V)	Analog Read Value
0V	0
2.5V	512
5V	1023

2. How to Read an Analog Input

To read an **analog sensor** or **potentiometer**, follow these steps:

1. **Connect the sensor output to an analog pin (A0–A5).**
2. **Use analogRead(pin) to get a value between 0 and 1023.**
3. **Convert this value to useful units (e.g., voltage or temperature).**

3. Example: Reading a Potentiometer (Variable Resistor)

A **potentiometer** is a knob that changes resistance when turned. You can use it to control volume, brightness, or speed.

Wiring:

- **Middle pin** → Connect to **A0**

- **Left pin** → Connect to **5V**

- **Right pin** → Connect to **GND**

Code: Reading a Potentiometer

```
int potPin = A0;   // Potentiometer connected to A0

int potValue;       // Variable to store the reading


void setup() {

  Serial.begin(9600);   // Start Serial Monitor

}


void loop() {

  potValue = analogRead(potPin);   // Read analog value (0-1023)

  Serial.println(potValue);          // Print value to Serial Monitor

  delay(500);   // Wait 500ms before reading again

}
```

◆ **How It Works:**

✓ analogRead(potPin); – Reads the analog voltage from the potentiometer.

✓ Serial.println(potValue); – Displays the value in the **Serial Monitor**.

4. Example: Reading a Light Sensor (LDR - Light Dependent Resistor)

A **Light Dependent Resistor (LDR)** changes resistance based on light intensity. It can be used for **automatic lighting** or **light-sensitive alarms**.

Wiring:

- **One side** → **5V**

- **Other side** → A1 and a **10kΩ resistor** to **GND**

Code: Reading a Light Sensor

```
int ldrPin = A1;   // LDR connected to A1
```

```
int lightValue;    // Variable to store reading


void setup() {

  Serial.begin(9600);

}


void loop() {

  lightValue = analogRead(ldrPin);   // Read light level

  Serial.println(lightValue);        // Print value

  delay(500);

}
```

◆ **How It Works:**

✓ Higher values mean **brighter light**.

✓ Lower values mean **darker environment**.

5. Summary: How to Read Analog Inputs

✓ **Analog inputs measure varying voltages (0V to 5V).**

✓ Use **pins A0–A5 for sensors, potentiometers, and other analog devices.**

✓ Use **analogRead(pin)** to get a value from **0 to 1023**.

✓ Convert the reading into meaningful values (e.g., light level, temperature).

With this knowledge, you can now start working with **temperature sensors, sound sensors, and more**!

Using potentiometers and sensors

Potentiometers and sensors allow your **Arduino Nano** to interact with the environment by measuring **light, temperature, sound, motion, and more**. They provide **analog input values** that can be used to control devices like LEDs, motors, and displays.

1. What is a Potentiometer?

A **potentiometer** (or "pot") is a **variable resistor** that changes its resistance when you turn a knob. It is commonly used to adjust volume, brightness, or speed.

How It Works:

- One pin connects to **5V** (power).

- One pin connects to **GND** (ground).

- The middle pin connects to an **analog input (A0–A5)** and outputs a voltage between **0V and 5V**.

Example: Reading a Potentiometer

Wiring:

- **Left pin → 5V**

- **Middle pin → A0**

- **Right pin → GND**

Code: Reading a Potentiometer and Printing the Value

```
int potPin = A0;   // Potentiometer connected to A0

int potValue;      // Store the value


void setup() {

  Serial.begin(9600);  // Start Serial Monitor

}


void loop() {

  potValue = analogRead(potPin);  // Read the value (0-1023)

  Serial.println(potValue);       // Print value to Serial Monitor

  delay(500);
```

```
}
```

◆ **What Happens?**
✓ The **Serial Monitor** displays a value between **0 and 1023**.
✓ Turning the knob **left decreases the value**, and turning it **right increases the value**.

2. Using Sensors with Arduino

Arduino can read values from many **analog sensors**, such as:
✓ **Light sensors (LDR - Light Dependent Resistor)** → Detects brightness.
✓ **Temperature sensors (e.g., LM35, DHT11)** → Measures heat.
✓ **Sound sensors (microphones)** → Detects noise levels.

Example: Reading a Light Sensor (LDR)

Wiring:

- **One side of the LDR → 5V**

- **Other side → A1 and a 10kΩ resistor** to GND

Code: Measuring Light Intensity

```
int ldrPin = A1;   // LDR connected to A1

int lightValue;    // Store the reading


void setup() {

  Serial.begin(9600);  // Start Serial Monitor

}


void loop() {

  lightValue = analogRead(ldrPin);  // Read LDR value

  Serial.println(lightValue);       // Print value

  delay(500);

}
```

◆ **How It Works:**

✓ Bright light → **High values** (close to 1023).

✓ Dark room → **Low values** (close to 0).

3. Controlling an LED with a Potentiometer

We can use a potentiometer to **adjust LED brightness** based on the input value.

Wiring:

- **Potentiometer middle pin → A0**

- **LED → Pin 9 (PWM pin)**

- **Resistor (220Ω) → Between LED and GND**

Code: Adjust LED Brightness with Potentiometer

```
int potPin = A0;

int ledPin = 9;

int potValue;


void setup() {

  pinMode(ledPin, OUTPUT);

}


void loop() {

  potValue = analogRead(potPin); // Read potentiometer

  int brightness = map(potValue, 0, 1023, 0, 255); //
Convert range

  analogWrite(ledPin, brightness); // Adjust LED
brightness

}
```

◆ **How It Works:**

✓ Turning the knob **changes LED brightness** from **dim to bright**.

✓ The map() function converts **0-1023 (potentiometer range)** to **0-255 (PWM LED brightness range)**.

4. Summary: Using Potentiometers and Sensors

✓ **Potentiometers** provide an adjustable voltage to control devices.
✓ **Analog sensors** measure real-world conditions like light and temperature.
✓ **analogRead(pin)** reads values from **0 to 1023**.
✓ **Mapped values** can be used to control LEDs, motors, or displays.

With these concepts, you can start creating **interactive projects** like automatic lighting, sound-reactive LEDs, or temperature-controlled fans!

Generating analog outputs with PWM

The **Arduino Nano** does not have a true **analog output**, but it can simulate one using **Pulse Width Modulation (PWM)**. PWM allows you to control the brightness of LEDs, adjust motor speed, and create smooth fading effects.

1. What is PWM (Pulse Width Modulation)?

PWM works by rapidly switching a pin between HIGH (5V) and LOW (0V) at a high frequency. By changing the amount of time the pin stays **HIGH vs. LOW**, we can control the output **power level**.

✓ **If HIGH for more time** → More power (brighter LED, faster motor).
✓ **If LOW for more time** → Less power (dim LED, slower motor).

This is measured as a **duty cycle** (percentage of time the signal is HIGH in one cycle).

Duty Cycle (%)	LED Brightness	Motor Speed
0% (LOW all time)	Off	Stopped
50% (Equal HIGH & LOW)	Half-bright	Medium speed
100% (HIGH all time)	Full brightness	Full speed

2. Using analogWrite() for PWM Output

Arduino has **6 PWM pins** (marked with ~):
✦ **PWM pins on Arduino Nano: D3, D5, D6, D9, D10, D11**

Use **analogWrite(pin, value)** to set the PWM level:

✓ value = 0 (0% duty cycle) → Output is **LOW (0V)**.

✓ value = 255 (100% duty cycle) → Output is **HIGH (5V)**.

✓ value = 127 (50% duty cycle) → Output is **2.5V**.

3. Example: Fading an LED Using PWM

We can gradually **increase and decrease the brightness** of an LED using PWM.

Wiring:

- **LED → Pin 9 (PWM pin)**

- **Resistor (220Ω) → Between LED and GND**

Code: LED Fading Effect

```
int ledPin = 9;  // LED connected to PWM pin 9


void setup() {
  pinMode(ledPin, OUTPUT);
}


void loop() {
  // Increase brightness
  for (int brightness = 0; brightness <= 255;
brightness++) {
    analogWrite(ledPin, brightness);
    delay(10);  // Short delay to create fading effect
  }


  // Decrease brightness
  for (int brightness = 255; brightness >= 0; brightness--
) {
    analogWrite(ledPin, brightness);
```

```
   delay(10);
  }

}
```

◆ **How It Works:**

✓ **Loop increases PWM value** from **0 to 255** (LED brightens).

✓ **Loop decreases PWM value** from **255 to 0** (LED dims).

✓ **analogWrite(ledPin, brightness);** controls brightness smoothly.

4. Controlling Motor Speed with PWM

PWM can also control **DC motors** by adjusting power levels.

Wiring:

- **Motor driver (e.g., L298N or transistor) → PWM Pin 6**

- **Motor → Motor driver output**

Code: Adjust Motor Speed

```
int motorPin = 6;  // Motor connected to PWM pin 6


void setup() {
  pinMode(motorPin, OUTPUT);
}


void loop() {
  analogWrite(motorPin, 128);  // Set motor speed to 50%
power
  delay(2000);
  analogWrite(motorPin, 255);  // Full speed
  delay(2000);
  analogWrite(motorPin, 0);    // Stop motor
  delay(2000);
```

```
}
```

◆ **How It Works:**

✓ **PWM value 0** → Motor is **off**.

✓ **PWM value 128 (50%)** → Motor runs at **half speed**.

✓ **PWM value 255 (100%)** → Motor runs at **full speed**.

5. Summary: Generating Analog Outputs with PWM

✓ **PWM simulates an analog output using fast switching**.

✓ **Use analogWrite(pin, value);** to control **brightness or speed**.

✓ **Arduino Nano supports PWM on Pins 3, 5, 6, 9, 10, 11**.

✓ **Useful for LED dimming, motor control, and audio signals**.

Now that you understand PWM, you can start making **interactive lighting effects, motor speed controllers, and more!**

Serial Communication

Understanding serial communication

Serial communication allows your **Arduino Nano** to **send and receive data** between the **Arduino board and a computer, another microcontroller, or external devices** like sensors and displays. This is one of the most important ways to debug, monitor, and control your projects.

1. What is Serial Communication?

Serial communication is a way of **transmitting data one bit at a time** over a communication channel. It is used to exchange data between devices using just **two wires**:

✓ **TX (Transmit)** → Sends data **from** Arduino **to another device**.
✓ **RX (Receive)** → Receives data **from another device to Arduino**.

On the **Arduino Nano**, the serial communication pins are:
✦ **TX (Transmit)** → **Pin 1**
✦ **RX (Receive)** → **Pin 0**

◆ However, the **USB cable** connected to your computer also uses serial communication, so you can send and receive data through the **Serial Monitor** in the Arduino IDE.

2. How Serial Communication Works on Arduino

Arduino uses a built-in **hardware serial port** that communicates at different **baud rates** (data transfer speeds). The most commonly used speed is **9600 baud**, meaning **9600 bits per second**.

To enable serial communication in Arduino, use:

```
Serial.begin(9600);  // Start serial communication at 9600
baud
```

◆ **Baud Rate Options:**

Baud Rate	Data Speed (bits per second)
9600	Standard speed (most common)

Baud Rate	Data Speed (bits per second)
115200	Faster data transfer
57600	Medium speed

Both devices communicating must use the **same baud rate** to understand each other.

3. Simple Serial Communication Example

The following code starts serial communication and **sends a message** to the **Serial Monitor** every second.

```
void setup() {

  Serial.begin(9600);  // Initialize serial communication

}


void loop() {

  Serial.println("Hello, Arduino!");  // Send a message

  delay(1000);  // Wait 1 second

}
```

◆ **What Happens?**

✓ The **Arduino sends "Hello, Arduino!"** every second.

✓ You can view the messages in the **Serial Monitor** in the Arduino IDE.

4. Why is Serial Communication Useful?

✓ **Debugging** → Print messages to check if your code is working.

✓ **Monitoring Sensors** → Read and display sensor data in real-time.

✓ **Sending Commands** → Control the Arduino from a computer or another device.

✓ **Connecting External Devices** → Communicate with GPS, WiFi, and Bluetooth modules.

Summary: What You Learned

✔ **Serial communication** allows data transfer between devices using TX and RX pins.

✔ The **Arduino Nano** communicates over USB using the **Serial Monitor**.

✔ **Serial.begin(9600);** starts serial communication at **9600 baud**.

✔ **Useful for debugging, monitoring, and controlling devices**.

Now that you understand serial communication, you can start **sending and receiving data** from your Arduino Nano to make your projects more interactive!

Communicating with the serial monitor

The **Serial Monitor** in the Arduino IDE is a powerful tool that allows you to **send and receive data between your Arduino Nano and your computer**. It is commonly used for **debugging, monitoring sensor values, and sending commands to the Arduino**.

1. What is the Serial Monitor?

The **Serial Monitor** is a built-in tool in the Arduino IDE that displays messages sent by the Arduino using Serial.print() or Serial.println(). It also allows you to **send data back to the Arduino**, making it interactive.

✔ **Displays messages from the Arduino** (useful for debugging).

✔ **Shows real-time sensor readings and values**.

✔ **Allows you to send commands to the Arduino** (e.g., turn LEDs on/off).

2. How to Open the Serial Monitor

Steps:

1. Open the **Arduino IDE**.
2. Click on **Tools → Serial Monitor** (or press Ctrl + Shift + M).
3. Set the **baud rate** (must match Serial.begin(baudRate); in your code).

◆ A window will open, displaying data sent from the Arduino. You can also type and send messages back to the Arduino using the input box.

3. Sending Messages from Arduino to Serial Monitor

To send messages to the Serial Monitor, use **Serial.print()** or **Serial.println()**.

Example: Sending a Message Every Second

```
void setup() {
```

```
  Serial.begin(9600);  // Start Serial Monitor at 9600
baud

}
```

```
void loop() {

  Serial.println("Hello from Arduino!");  // Send message

  delay(1000);  // Wait 1 second

}
```

✓ Serial.println("Hello from Arduino!"); → Sends text to the Serial Monitor with a new line.
✓ Serial.print("Hello"); → Sends text without a new line (useful for formatting).

4. Displaying Sensor Readings in the Serial Monitor

Let's read a **potentiometer value** and display it in the Serial Monitor.

Wiring:

- **Potentiometer middle pin → A0**

- **One side → 5V**

- **Other side → GND**

Code: Reading a Potentiometer and Displaying It

```
int potPin = A0;  // Potentiometer connected to A0


void setup() {

  Serial.begin(9600);  // Start Serial Monitor

}


void loop() {

  int value = analogRead(potPin);  // Read potentiometer
```

```
Serial.print("Potentiometer Value: ");

Serial.println(value);  // Print value with a new line

delay(500);
}
```

◆ **What Happens?**
✓ Turning the knob **changes the values** printed in the Serial Monitor.
✓ Values range **from 0 (0V) to 1023 (5V)**.

5. Sending Data to Arduino from the Serial Monitor

You can also **send messages to Arduino** from the Serial Monitor.

Example: Turn an LED On/Off Using Serial Input

Wiring:

- **LED → Pin 13**

- **Resistor (220Ω) → Between LED and GND**

Code: Controlling an LED from Serial Monitor

```
int ledPin = 13;


void setup() {

  Serial.begin(9600);  // Start Serial Monitor

  pinMode(ledPin, OUTPUT);
}


void loop() {

  if (Serial.available()) {  // Check if data is received

    char command = Serial.read();  // Read the input

    if (command == '1') {

      digitalWrite(ledPin, HIGH);  // Turn LED on
```

```
      Serial.println("LED ON");

   } else if (command == '0') {

      digitalWrite(ledPin, LOW);  // Turn LED off

      Serial.println("LED OFF");

   }

 }

}
```

◆ **How It Works:**
✓ Open the Serial Monitor, type **1**, and press **Enter** → **LED turns ON**.
✓ Type **0** and press **Enter** → **LED turns OFF**.
✓ Serial.available() checks if data is received.
✓ Serial.read() reads the input character.

6. Summary: Using the Serial Monitor

✓ **The Serial Monitor lets you send and receive data with Arduino.**
✓ **Use Serial.println() to display text or sensor values.**
✓ **You can control Arduino by sending commands through the Serial Monitor.**
✓ **Great for debugging, testing, and interacting with your projects!**

Now that you know how to use the Serial Monitor, you can start building **interactive projects** where Arduino responds to commands from your computer!

Sending and receiving data

Serial communication allows your **Arduino Nano** to send and receive data between your computer, other microcontrollers, or external devices. This is useful for **monitoring sensor values, controlling components, and debugging your projects**.

1. Sending Data from Arduino to a Computer

You can send data to your computer using **Serial.print()** or **Serial.println()**.

Example: Sending Text to the Serial Monitor

```
void setup() {
```

```
  Serial.begin(9600);   // Start serial communication at
9600 baud

}


void loop() {

  Serial.println("Hello, Arduino!");   // Send text to
Serial Monitor

  delay(1000);   // Wait 1 second

}
```

◆ **What Happens?**

✓ The **Arduino sends "Hello, Arduino!" every second** to the Serial Monitor.

✓ Serial.println() adds a **new line** after each message.

2. Sending Sensor Data from Arduino

Let's send **sensor values** to the Serial Monitor.

Example: Reading and Sending a Potentiometer Value

Wiring:

- **Potentiometer middle pin → A0**

- **One side → 5V**

- **Other side → GND**

Code: Sending Sensor Data

```
int potPin = A0;   // Potentiometer connected to A0


void setup() {

  Serial.begin(9600);   // Start serial communication

}


void loop() {
```

```
int value = analogRead(potPin);   // Read potentiometer

Serial.print("Potentiometer Value: ");

Serial.println(value);   // Send value to Serial Monitor

delay(500);
}
```

◆ **What Happens?**

✓ Turning the knob **changes the value** displayed in the Serial Monitor.

✓ Values range from **0 (0V) to 1023 (5V)**.

3. Receiving Data from a Computer to Arduino

You can send commands from your computer to control the **Arduino Nano** using the **Serial Monitor**.

Example: Turning an LED On/Off Using Serial Input

Wiring:

- **LED → Pin 13**

- **Resistor (220Ω) → Between LED and GND**

Code: Receiving Data to Control an LED

```
int ledPin = 13;


void setup() {

  Serial.begin(9600);   // Start Serial Monitor

  pinMode(ledPin, OUTPUT);
}


void loop() {

  if (Serial.available()) {   // Check if data is received

    char command = Serial.read();   // Read the input

    if (command == '1') {
```

```
    digitalWrite(ledPin, HIGH);  // Turn LED on

    Serial.println("LED ON");

  } else if (command == '0') {

    digitalWrite(ledPin, LOW);  // Turn LED off

    Serial.println("LED OFF");

  }

 }

}
```

◆ **How It Works:**

✓ Open the Serial Monitor, type **1**, and press **Enter** → **LED turns ON**.

✓ Type **0** and press **Enter** → **LED turns OFF**.

✓ Serial.available() checks if data is received.

✓ Serial.read() reads the input character.

4. Two-Way Communication: Sending and Receiving Data

In some projects, you might want **Arduino to send sensor data** and **receive user commands at the same time.**

Example: Controlling an LED and Showing Sensor Data

```
int potPin = A0;

int ledPin = 13;

int potValue;


void setup() {

  Serial.begin(9600);

  pinMode(ledPin, OUTPUT);

}


void loop() {

  potValue = analogRead(potPin);  // Read sensor value
```

```
  Serial.print("Potentiometer: ");

  Serial.println(potValue);


  if (Serial.available()) {

    char command = Serial.read();

    if (command == '1') {

      digitalWrite(ledPin, HIGH);

      Serial.println("LED ON");

    } else if (command == '0') {

      digitalWrite(ledPin, LOW);

      Serial.println("LED OFF");

    }

  }

  delay(500);

}
```

◆ **What Happens?**

✓ Arduino **sends sensor data** every 500ms.

✓ User **sends "1" or "0" to control the LED**.

5. Summary: Sending and Receiving Data

✓ **Serial.print() and Serial.println()** send data to the Serial Monitor.

✓ **Serial.read() reads incoming data from the user.**

✓ **Serial.available() checks if data is received.**

✓ You can create **interactive projects** by sending and receiving data between your computer and Arduino!

Now you're ready to build **real-time interactive Arduino projects** using serial communication!

Control Structures and Functions

Using loops and conditional statements

In Arduino programming, **loops** and **conditional statements** help control how your program runs. Loops allow you to **repeat actions**, while conditional statements let your Arduino **make decisions** based on input values.

1. Using Loops in Arduino

Loops help you run a block of code **multiple times** instead of writing the same code over and over.

(A) for Loop – Repeating a Task a Fixed Number of Times

A for loop repeats code **a specific number of times**. It is commonly used for controlling LEDs, motors, and other repetitive actions.

Example: Blinking an LED 5 Times

```
int ledPin = 13;


void setup() {
  pinMode(ledPin, OUTPUT);
}


void loop() {
  for (int i = 0; i < 5; i++) {  // Repeat 5 times
    digitalWrite(ledPin, HIGH);
    delay(500);
    digitalWrite(ledPin, LOW);
    delay(500);
  }
  delay(2000);  // Wait before repeating
```

```
}
```

✓ The LED **blinks 5 times**, then pauses for **2 seconds** before repeating.
✓ for (int i = 0; i < 5; i++) means **start at 0, repeat 5 times, increasing by 1 each time**.

(B) while Loop – Repeating Until a Condition is Met

A while loop runs **as long as a condition is true**. This is useful for **waiting for a button press** or **monitoring sensor values**.

Example: Wait for a Button Press

```
int buttonPin = 2;


void setup() {

  pinMode(buttonPin, INPUT_PULLUP);

  Serial.begin(9600);

}


void loop() {

  while (digitalRead(buttonPin) == HIGH) {   // Wait until button is pressed

    Serial.println("Waiting for button press...");

    delay(500);

  }

  Serial.println("Button pressed!");

}
```

✓ The program keeps printing **"Waiting for button press..."** until you press the button.
✓ Once the button is pressed, it prints **"Button pressed!"** and exits the loop.

(C) do...while Loop – Always Runs at Least Once

A do...while loop is similar to a while loop, but it **always runs at least once**, even if the condition is false.

Example: Reading User Input

```
char input;


void setup() {
  Serial.begin(9600);
}


void loop() {
  do {
    Serial.println("Press 'y' to continue...");
    delay(1000);
  } while (Serial.available() == 0);   // Wait for user
input


  input = Serial.read();
  Serial.print("You pressed: ");
  Serial.println(input);
}
```

✓ The message **"Press 'y' to continue..."** is printed **at least once** before checking input.

2. Using Conditional Statements in Arduino

Conditional statements allow your Arduino to **make decisions** based on **sensor readings, button presses, or other inputs**.

(A) if Statement – Runs Code When a Condition is True

An if statement **checks a condition** and runs code only if it's true.

Example: Turn an LED On When a Button is Pressed

```
int buttonPin = 2;

int ledPin = 13;


void setup() {

  pinMode(buttonPin, INPUT_PULLUP);

  pinMode(ledPin, OUTPUT);

}


void loop() {

  if (digitalRead(buttonPin) == LOW) {  // Button is pressed

    digitalWrite(ledPin, HIGH);  // Turn LED on

  } else {

    digitalWrite(ledPin, LOW);  // Turn LED off

  }

}
```

✓ If the button is **pressed**, the LED turns **on**.
✓ If the button is **not pressed**, the LED stays **off**.

(B) if...else Statement – Choosing Between Two Actions

If you need to **choose between two different actions**, use if...else.

Example: Adjust LED Brightness Based on Sensor Input

```
int sensorPin = A0;

int ledPin = 9;


void setup() {

  pinMode(ledPin, OUTPUT);
```

```
  Serial.begin(9600);

}


void loop() {

  int sensorValue = analogRead(sensorPin);


  if (sensorValue > 512) {

    analogWrite(ledPin, 255);  // Full brightness

    Serial.println("Bright light detected!");

  } else {

    analogWrite(ledPin, 50);  // Dim light

    Serial.println("Low light detected.");

  }

}
```

✓ If the **sensor value is above 512**, the LED is **bright**.
✓ If the **sensor value is below 512**, the LED is **dim**.

(C) switch...case – Handling Multiple Conditions

If you have **multiple conditions**, a switch...case is often better than multiple if statements.

Example: Control an LED Mode with Serial Input

```
int ledPin = 9;


void setup() {

  pinMode(ledPin, OUTPUT);

  Serial.begin(9600);

}
```

```
void loop() {
  if (Serial.available()) {
    char command = Serial.read();

    switch (command) {
      case '1':
        analogWrite(ledPin, 255);  // Full brightness
        Serial.println("LED Full Brightness");
        break;
      case '2':
        analogWrite(ledPin, 128);  // Medium brightness
        Serial.println("LED Medium Brightness");
        break;
      case '3':
        analogWrite(ledPin, 50);  // Low brightness
        Serial.println("LED Low Brightness");
        break;
      default:
        analogWrite(ledPin, 0);  // Turn off LED
        Serial.println("LED OFF");
    }
  }
}
```

✓ Type '1', '2', or '3' in the Serial Monitor to change LED brightness.
✓ If an unknown value is received, the LED turns off.

3. Summary: Loops and Conditional Statements in Arduino

✓ Loops:

- for → Repeats a task **a set number of times**.

- while → Runs as long as **a condition is true**.

- do...while → Always runs **at least once**, then checks the condition.

✓ Conditional Statements:

- if → Runs code **if a condition is true**.

- if...else → Chooses **between two actions**.

- switch...case → Best for **multiple conditions** (e.g., menu selection).

Now you can use **loops to automate tasks** and **conditional statements to make decisions**, giving you full control over your Arduino projects!

Creating and using functions

Functions are one of the most important features in **Arduino programming**. They allow you to **organize your code**, make it **easier to read**, and **reuse blocks of code** without writing them multiple times.

1. What is a Function?

A **function** is a reusable block of code that performs a specific task. Instead of writing the same code over and over, you can **write a function once and call it whenever needed**.

Every Arduino program already has two built-in functions:

```
void setup() {

  // Runs once at the beginning

}
```

```
void loop() {

  // Repeats continuously

}
```

But you can also **create your own functions** to organize your program better!

2. How to Create a Function in Arduino

A function in Arduino consists of **three parts**:

```
returnType functionName(parameters) {

  // Code that runs when the function is called

  return value;  // (Optional) Returns a value

}
```

✓ **returnType** – The type of value the function returns (void if it returns nothing).
✓ **functionName** – The name of the function (choose something meaningful).
✓ **parameters** – Optional inputs the function can use.
✓ **return value;** – Optional; returns a result if needed.

3. Example: Creating a Simple Function

Let's create a function that **blinks an LED**.

Code: Function to Blink an LED

```
void blinkLED() {

  digitalWrite(13, HIGH);  // Turn LED on

  delay(500);              // Wait 500ms

  digitalWrite(13, LOW);   // Turn LED off

  delay(500);

}


void setup() {

  pinMode(13, OUTPUT);

}


void loop() {
```

```
   blinkLED();  // Call the function

}
```

♦ **What Happens?**

✓ The function blinkLED() **turns the LED on and off**.

✓ In loop(), calling blinkLED(); makes the LED blink continuously.

4. Passing Parameters to a Function

Functions can **accept values (parameters)** to make them more flexible.

Code: Function to Blink an LED with a Custom Delay

```
void blinkLED(int delayTime) {

   digitalWrite(13, HIGH);

   delay(delayTime);

   digitalWrite(13, LOW);

   delay(delayTime);

}


void setup() {

   pinMode(13, OUTPUT);

}


void loop() {

   blinkLED(200);  // Call function with a 200ms delay

   blinkLED(500);  // Call function with a 500ms delay

}
```

♦ **What Happens?**

✓ The LED blinks **at two different speeds** because we call the function with different delay times.

✓ blinkLED(200); → Blinks fast, blinkLED(500); → Blinks slower.

5. Returning a Value from a Function

Some functions **return a value** after performing a calculation.

Code: Function to Double a Number

```
int doubleNumber(int num) {

  return num * 2;  // Multiply the number by 2 and return
the result

}


void setup() {

  Serial.begin(9600);

}


void loop() {

  int result = doubleNumber(5);  // Call function and
store result

  Serial.println(result);  // Print result (10)

  delay(1000);

}
```

◆ **What Happens?**

✓ The function doubleNumber(5); **returns 10**.

✓ The result is printed in the **Serial Monitor**.

6. Combining Functions for Better Code Structure

Instead of writing everything in loop(), you can **break down your program into smaller functions** for better readability.

Example: Organizing an LED Control Program

```
int ledPin = 9;


void setup() {

  pinMode(ledPin, OUTPUT);
```

```
  Serial.begin(9600);
}


void loop() {
  int brightness = readSensor();
  controlLED(brightness);
  delay(500);
}


// Function to read a sensor value
int readSensor() {
  int value = analogRead(A0);
  Serial.print("Sensor Value: ");
  Serial.println(value);
  return value;
}


// Function to control LED brightness based on sensor
input
void controlLED(int sensorValue) {
  int brightness = map(sensorValue, 0, 1023, 0, 255);
  analogWrite(ledPin, brightness);
}
```

◆ **What Happens?**

✓ The readSensor() function reads a **sensor value** and prints it.

✓ The controlLED() function adjusts the **LED brightness** based on the sensor reading.

✓ The loop() function stays **clean and readable**.

7. Summary: Why Use Functions?

✓ **Avoid repetition** – Write code once and reuse it.
✓ **Improve readability** – Makes programs easier to understand.
✓ **Make debugging easier** – Easier to find and fix errors.
✓ **Enable modular coding** – You can reuse functions in other projects.

Now that you know how to create and use functions, you can **write cleaner, more efficient Arduino programs**!

Modularizing your code for readability

Modular programming is a way of **breaking your code into smaller, reusable functions** to make it easier to read, understand, and maintain. Instead of writing everything in loop(), you can **divide your program into clear sections** that perform specific tasks.

1. Why Modular Code is Important

✓ **Easier to Read** – When code is well-organized, it's easier to follow.
✓ **Reusable Functions** – Functions can be used in different parts of the program.
✓ **Easier Debugging** – If something doesn't work, you can check one function instead of searching the whole program.
✓ **Better Collaboration** – If multiple people work on a project, modular code helps them understand different parts easily.

2. Example of Unstructured (Messy) Code

Here's an example of **poorly structured code** that does too much inside loop():

```
int sensorPin = A0;

int ledPin = 9;


void setup() {

  pinMode(ledPin, OUTPUT);

  Serial.begin(9600);

}
```

```
void loop() {
  int sensorValue = analogRead(sensorPin);
  Serial.print("Sensor Value: ");
  Serial.println(sensorValue);

  int brightness = map(sensorValue, 0, 1023, 0, 255);
  analogWrite(ledPin, brightness);

  delay(500);
}
```

● **Problem**: Everything is in loop(), making it harder to read and modify.

---

3. Modularizing the Code

We can improve the readability by **splitting the code into separate functions**.

Refactored (Modular) Code

```
int sensorPin = A0;
int ledPin = 9;

void setup() {
  pinMode(ledPin, OUTPUT);
  Serial.begin(9600);
}

void loop() {
  int sensorValue = readSensor();
  controlLED(sensorValue);
```

```
  delay(500);
}


// Function to read a sensor value
int readSensor() {
  int value = analogRead(sensorPin);
  Serial.print("Sensor Value: ");
  Serial.println(value);
  return value;
}


// Function to control LED brightness based on sensor
input
void controlLED(int sensorValue) {
  int brightness = map(sensorValue, 0, 1023, 0, 255);
  analogWrite(ledPin, brightness);
}
```

✅ **Improvements:**
✔ readSensor() – Handles **reading and printing sensor values**.
✔ controlLED() – Handles **adjusting the LED brightness**.
✔ loop() – Now only calls these functions, making it **clean and easy to read**.

4. Using Header Files for Large Projects

For **larger projects**, you can **separate functions into different files** to keep your main program clean.

Example: Creating a Header File (led_control.h)

1. **Create a new file named** led_control.h.
2. **Move LED-related functions into it:**

```
#ifndef LED_CONTROL_H
```

```
#define LED_CONTROL_H

void controlLED(int sensorValue) {
  int brightness = map(sensorValue, 0, 1023, 0, 255);
  analogWrite(9, brightness);
}


#endif
```

3. **In your main Arduino file (sketch.ino)**, include the header:

```
#include "led_control.h"

int sensorPin = A0;

void setup() {
  pinMode(9, OUTPUT);
  Serial.begin(9600);
}


void loop() {
  int sensorValue = analogRead(sensorPin);
  controlLED(sensorValue);
  delay(500);
}
```

✓ Now **LED control is separate**, and the main file remains **clean**.

5. Summary: How to Modularize Your Code

✓ **Use functions** to separate tasks (**readSensor(), controlLED()**).

✓ **Keep loop() simple** by calling functions instead of writing everything inside it.

✓ **Use header files (.h)** for large projects to organize code.

✓ **Write reusable functions** to avoid repeating code.

By following these principles, your Arduino projects will be **cleaner, more readable, and easier to expand**!

Arrays and Data Management

Understanding arrays

An **array** is a way to store **multiple values** in a **single variable**. Instead of creating separate variables for each value, an array lets you **group related data together**. This makes your code **simpler, more efficient, and easier to manage**.

1. Why Use Arrays?

✓ **Store multiple values** in a single variable.
✓ **Easier to manage** than multiple separate variables.
✓ **Loop through values** instead of writing repetitive code.
✓ **Useful for storing sensor readings, LED states, button presses, etc.**

2. Declaring an Array

To create an array in Arduino, use this format:

```
dataType arrayName[size] = {value1, value2, value3, ...};
```

✓ **dataType** – The type of data (e.g., int, float, char).
✓ **arrayName** – The name of the array.
✓ **size** – The number of elements in the array.
✓ **Values** – The values stored in the array.

3. Example: Storing LED Pins in an Array

Instead of writing separate variables for each **LED pin**, we can store them in an array:

```
int ledPins[3] = {3, 5, 9};  // Store three LED pins in an array


void setup() {
  for (int i = 0; i < 3; i++) {  // Loop through the array
    pinMode(ledPins[i], OUTPUT);
  }
}
```

```
void loop() {
  for (int i = 0; i < 3; i++) {
    digitalWrite(ledPins[i], HIGH);  // Turn each LED on
    delay(500);
    digitalWrite(ledPins[i], LOW);   // Turn each LED off
    delay(500);
  }
}
```

◆ **What Happens?**

✓ The program **loops through the array** to control the LEDs.

✓ Using ledPins[i] replaces the need for multiple variables.

4. Accessing Array Elements

Each value in an array has an **index number** (position). **Indexing starts from 0,** not 1.

```
int numbers[4] = {10, 20, 30, 40};
```

```
Serial.println(numbers[0]);  // Prints 10

Serial.println(numbers[1]);  // Prints 20

Serial.println(numbers[2]);  // Prints 30

Serial.println(numbers[3]);  // Prints 40
```

✓ numbers[0] is the **first element** (10).

✓ numbers[3] is the **last element** (40).

5. Changing Values in an Array

You can **modify** array values by assigning new data.

```
int scores[3] = {80, 90, 100};

scores[1] = 95;  // Change second element from 90 to 95
```

Now, scores[1] will return **95** instead of **90**.

6. Using Arrays with Sensors

You can use arrays to **store multiple sensor readings** and process them.

Example: Storing Temperature Readings

```
int temperatures[5];   // Array to store 5 readings

int sensorPin = A0;


void setup() {

  Serial.begin(9600);

}


void loop() {

  for (int i = 0; i < 5; i++) {

    temperatures[i] = analogRead(sensorPin);   // Store
sensor value

    Serial.print("Reading ");

    Serial.print(i);

    Serial.print(": ");

    Serial.println(temperatures[i]);   // Print each
reading

    delay(1000);

  }

}
```

◆ **What Happens?**
✓ The program **reads and stores 5 temperature values**.
✓ Each value is printed with its **position in the array**.

7. Summary: Why Use Arrays?

✓ **Arrays store multiple values in one variable.**
✓ **Indexes start at 0**, and you access elements using array[index].
✓ **Looping through arrays makes code simpler** and avoids repetitive writing.
✓ **Great for handling multiple LEDs, sensors, and data storage**.

With arrays, you can **manage multiple values efficiently** and build **more advanced Arduino projects**!

Storing and manipulating data

In Arduino programming, you often need to **store, modify, and process multiple values** efficiently. Using **arrays and variables**, you can manage sensor readings, button states, LED sequences, and more.

1. Storing Data in Arrays

Arrays allow you to **store multiple values** in a **single variable**, making it easy to organize data.

Example: Storing Sensor Readings

```
int sensorValues[5];  // Array to store 5 sensor readings

int sensorPin = A0;


void setup() {

  Serial.begin(9600);

}


void loop() {

  for (int i = 0; i < 5; i++) {

    sensorValues[i] = analogRead(sensorPin);  // Store
sensor reading

    Serial.print("Reading ");

    Serial.print(i);
```

```
    Serial.print(": ");

    Serial.println(sensorValues[i]);   // Print stored
value

    delay(1000);

  }

}
```

◆ **What Happens?**

✓ The program **reads and stores 5 values** from the sensor.

✓ Each value is printed with its **position in the array**.

2. Modifying Array Values

You can **change values** stored in an array anytime.

Example: Changing LED Blink Delays

```
int blinkTimes[3] = {200, 500, 1000};   // Different blink
delays


void setup() {

  pinMode(13, OUTPUT);

}


void loop() {

  for (int i = 0; i < 3; i++) {

    digitalWrite(13, HIGH);

    delay(blinkTimes[i]);   // Use array values for delays

    digitalWrite(13, LOW);

    delay(blinkTimes[i]);

  }

}
```

◆ **What Happens?**
✓ The LED **blinks at different speeds** using values from blinkTimes[].
✓ You can change the values **without modifying multiple lines of code**.

3. Processing Data: Finding Maximum and Average

You can use loops to **analyze data stored in arrays**.

Example: Finding the Maximum Sensor Value

```
int sensorReadings[5] = {300, 450, 512, 600, 720};


void setup() {

  Serial.begin(9600);

  int maxValue = sensorReadings[0];


  for (int i = 1; i < 5; i++) {

    if (sensorReadings[i] > maxValue) {

      maxValue = sensorReadings[i];   // Update max value

    }

  }


  Serial.print("Maximum Value: ");

  Serial.println(maxValue);

}


void loop() {}
```

◆ **What Happens?**
✓ The program **searches for the highest number** in the array.
✓ It prints the **maximum sensor value** in the Serial Monitor.

Example: Calculating the Average Value

```
int numbers[5] = {10, 20, 30, 40, 50};


void setup() {

  Serial.begin(9600);

  int sum = 0;


  for (int i = 0; i < 5; i++) {

    sum += numbers[i];   // Add up all values

  }


  int average = sum / 5;   // Calculate average

  Serial.print("Average Value: ");

  Serial.println(average);

}


void loop() {}
```

◆ What Happens?

✓ The program **calculates and prints the average** of the numbers in the array.

4. Sorting Data in an Array

Sorting helps **organize values** in ascending or descending order.

Example: Sorting Numbers in Ascending Order

```
int values[5] = {50, 10, 40, 20, 30};


void setup() {

  Serial.begin(9600);
```

```
// Bubble Sort Algorithm
for (int i = 0; i < 5; i++) {
  for (int j = 0; j < 4; j++) {
    if (values[j] > values[j + 1]) {
      int temp = values[j];
      values[j] = values[j + 1];
      values[j + 1] = temp;
    }
  }
}


Serial.println("Sorted Values:");
for (int i = 0; i < 5; i++) {
  Serial.println(values[i]);
}
}


void loop() {}
```

◆ **What Happens?**

✓ The numbers are **sorted from smallest to largest**.

✓ The sorted values are **printed in the Serial Monitor**.

5. Summary: How to Store and Manipulate Data in Arduino

✓ **Use arrays** to store multiple values efficiently.

✓ **Modify array values** dynamically during execution.

✓ **Use loops** to process data (find max, calculate average, etc.).

✓ **Sort arrays** to organize values in ascending or descending order.

By mastering data storage and manipulation, you can **create smarter Arduino projects** that analyze and process real-world data!

Practical applications in projects

Arrays and data management are essential in Arduino programming, allowing you to **store, process, and manipulate multiple values efficiently**. Below are some real-world projects where arrays and data handling make coding easier and more effective.

1. LED Light Sequences (Using Arrays for LED Patterns)

Arrays make it easy to control **multiple LEDs** in different patterns without repeating code.

Example: LED Chaser Effect

This project makes **LEDs light up one by one**, creating a moving effect.

Wiring:

- Connect **LEDs to Pins 3, 5, 6, 9, 10, and 11** with **220Ω resistors** to GND.

Code: LED Chaser Using an Array

```
int ledPins[6] = {3, 5, 6, 9, 10, 11};   // Store LED pins


void setup() {
  for (int i = 0; i < 6; i++) {
    pinMode(ledPins[i], OUTPUT);
  }
}


void loop() {
  for (int i = 0; i < 6; i++) {
    digitalWrite(ledPins[i], HIGH);   // Turn LED on
    delay(200);
    digitalWrite(ledPins[i], LOW);   // Turn LED off
```

```
    }
}
```

◆ **What Happens?**

✓ Each LED **lights up one after the other**, creating a **chaser effect**.

✓ The **array makes it easy to add or remove LEDs** without changing much code.

2. Storing and Processing Sensor Readings

Arrays are useful for storing **multiple sensor readings** and calculating useful statistics like the **average temperature, maximum light intensity, or noise levels**.

Example: Calculating the Average Temperature from Multiple Readings

Wiring:

- Connect a **temperature sensor (LM35)** to **A0**.

Code: Storing and Averaging Sensor Readings

```
int tempSensor = A0;

int readings[5];   // Store 5 temperature readings


void setup() {
  Serial.begin(9600);
}


void loop() {
  int sum = 0;


  for (int i = 0; i < 5; i++) {

    readings[i] = analogRead(tempSensor);   // Read
temperature sensor

    sum += readings[i];   // Add reading to sum
```

```
   delay(500);

 }


 int avgTemp = sum / 5;  // Calculate average

 Serial.print("Average Temperature: ");

 Serial.println(avgTemp);

}
```

◆ **What Happens?**

✓ The program **stores 5 temperature readings** and **calculates the average.**

✓ This prevents **sudden fluctuations** and provides a **more stable** reading.

3. Storing User Input (Keypad or Serial Data)

Arrays can store **user input from buttons, keypads, or serial communication.**

Example: Password Entry with a Keypad

A **4-digit password** must be entered to unlock a system.

```
char password[4] = {'1', '2', '3', '4'};  // Correct
password

char userInput[4];  // Store user input

int index = 0;


void setup() {

  Serial.begin(9600);

  Serial.println("Enter 4-digit password:");

}


void loop() {

  if (Serial.available()) {

    char key = Serial.read();  // Read input
```

```
userInput[index] = key;   // Store key in array
index++;


if (index == 4) {   // Check when 4 digits are entered
  if (memcmp(userInput, password, 4) == 0) {
    Serial.println("Access Granted!");
  } else {
    Serial.println("Incorrect Password!");
  }
  index = 0;   // Reset for next input
  }
 }
}
```

◆ **What Happens?**

✓ The user enters **a 4-digit password** via the **Serial Monitor**.

✓ The program **compares the input** with the correct password.

✓ If the password matches, it **grants access**; otherwise, it **denies access**.

4. Data Logging with SD Card Storage

Arrays help **store multiple sensor values** before writing them to an **SD card** for later analysis.

Example: Storing and Writing Temperature Data to an SD Card

Wiring:

- Connect an **SD card module** to **Arduino Nano (SPI pins)**.

Code: Logging Data to an SD Card

```
#include <SD.h>


const int chipSelect = 10;
```

```
int tempSensor = A0;

int tempReadings[5];


void setup() {

  Serial.begin(9600);

  SD.begin(chipSelect);

}


void loop() {

  File dataFile = SD.open("datalog.txt", FILE_WRITE);


  for (int i = 0; i < 5; i++) {

    tempReadings[i] = analogRead(tempSensor);

    dataFile.print("Temperature: ");

    dataFile.println(tempReadings[i]);

    delay(1000);

  }


  dataFile.close();

}
```

◆ **What Happens?**

✓ Sensor readings are stored in an **array** before writing to an **SD card**.

✓ This avoids writing data **one reading at a time**, reducing SD card wear.

5. Sorting and Filtering Sensor Data

You can **sort sensor data** to remove noise or detect trends, such as **finding the highest light level in a day**.

Example: Finding the Highest Light Level Recorded

```
int lightReadings[10] = {400, 350, 500, 450, 600, 520,
430, 480, 550, 530};

int highestValue = lightReadings[0];


void setup() {

  Serial.begin(9600);


  for (int i = 1; i < 10; i++) {

    if (lightReadings[i] > highestValue) {

      highestValue = lightReadings[i];

    }

  }


  Serial.print("Highest Light Level: ");

  Serial.println(highestValue);

}


void loop() {}
```

◆ **What Happens?**

✓ The program **scans an array of light readings**.

✓ It finds the **highest recorded value** and prints it.

6. Summary: Real-World Applications of Arrays and Data Management

✓ **LED Patterns** – Arrays make it easy to control **multiple LEDs**.

✓ **Sensor Data Processing** – Store and calculate **averages** for stable readings.

✓ **Password Entry** – Store and compare **user input**.

✓ **Data Logging** – Save sensor values on an **SD card**.

✓ **Sorting and Filtering** – Analyze **sensor trends** (highest, lowest, average values).

By mastering arrays and data management, you can **create complex Arduino projects** that store, process, and analyze information efficiently!

Libraries and Advanced Functions

Incorporating external libraries

Libraries are **pre-written code collections** that make programming easier by handling **complex tasks** like controlling sensors, displays, and communication modules. Instead of writing all the code from scratch, you can **use libraries to save time and simplify your projects**.

1. What is an Arduino Library?

✓ **A library is a set of ready-made functions** that you can use in your program.
✓ It helps you **control hardware easily** (like displays, sensors, and motors).
✓ Libraries are stored as **.h (header) and .cpp (code) files** inside the Arduino IDE.

2. How to Install a Library in Arduino IDE

You can install a library **in three ways**:

(A) Using the Library Manager (Recommended)

1. Open **Arduino IDE**.
2. Go to **Sketch → Include Library → Manage Libraries**.
3. In the search bar, type the library name (e.g., **LiquidCrystal** for LCDs).
4. Click **Install** and wait for the process to finish.

(B) Adding a ZIP Library (Downloaded Files)

1. Download the library as a **ZIP file** from sites like **GitHub** or **Arduino's official library page**.
2. Open **Arduino IDE**.
3. Go to **Sketch → Include Library → Add .ZIP Library**.
4. Select the downloaded ZIP file and click **Open**.

(C) Manually Copying Library Files

1. Download and extract the library folder.
2. Move the folder to **Documents → Arduino → Libraries**.
3. Restart the Arduino IDE to use the library.

3. Using an External Library in Your Code

Once installed, you need to **include the library in your sketch** using #include.

Example: Controlling an LCD with the LiquidCrystal Library

The **LiquidCrystal** library helps control **16x2 LCD screens** easily.

Wiring:

- RS → Pin 7, E → Pin 8, D4 → Pin 9, D5 → Pin 10, D6 → Pin 11, D7 → Pin 12

- VCC → 5V, GND → GND

Code: Displaying Text on an LCD

```
#include <LiquidCrystal.h>


// Define LCD pins: RS, E, D4, D5, D6, D7

LiquidCrystal lcd(7, 8, 9, 10, 11, 12);


void setup() {

  lcd.begin(16, 2);   // Set LCD size (16 columns, 2 rows)

  lcd.print("Hello, Arduino!");

}


void loop() {

}
```

◆ **What Happens?**
✓ The LCD screen displays **"Hello, Arduino!"**.
✓ The **LiquidCrystal library** simplifies working with LCDs.

4. Examples of Useful Libraries

Here are **popular Arduino libraries** and what they do:

Library Name	Functionality	Example Use
Wire.h	I2C communication	Read data from sensors like **MPU6050 (accelerometer)**
SPI.h	SPI communication	Control **SD cards** or **displays**
Servo.h	Servo motor control	Move **robot arms** or **servo motors**
DHT.h	Read temperature and humidity	Measure **room temperature** using **DHT11/DHT22 sensors**
Adafruit_GFX.h	Graphics for displays	Draw **shapes, text, and images** on OLED and TFT screens
SD.h	Read and write SD cards	Store **sensor data** on an SD card
AccelStepper.h	Control stepper motors	Create **CNC machines or robotic arms**

5. Example: Controlling a Servo Motor with the Servo Library

The **Servo.h** library makes it easy to control **servo motors** without writing complex code.

Wiring:

- **Servo Signal → Pin 9**

- **Servo VCC → 5V**

- **Servo GND → GND**

Code: Moving a Servo

```
#include <Servo.h>


Servo myServo;  // Create a servo object


void setup() {
```

```
  myServo.attach(9);  // Attach servo to pin 9
}


void loop() {
  myServo.write(0);   // Move to 0 degrees
  delay(1000);
  myServo.write(90);  // Move to 90 degrees
  delay(1000);
  myServo.write(180); // Move to 180 degrees
  delay(1000);
}
```

◈ **What Happens?**

✓ The **servo moves between 0°, 90°, and 180°**.

✓ The **Servo library** simplifies servo control.

6. Summary: Why Use Libraries?

✓ **Save time** – No need to write complex code from scratch.

✓ **Easy to use** – Simple functions for working with sensors, displays, and motors.

✓ **Expand Arduino capabilities** – Add new features like **WiFi, Bluetooth, or data storage**.

✓ **Many free libraries available** – Install from the **Arduino Library Manager** or GitHub.

By using external libraries, you can **build advanced Arduino projects** with **less effort and more functionality**!

Exploring advanced functions

In Arduino programming, **advanced functions** allow you to **optimize your code, handle complex tasks, and improve efficiency**. By using advanced functions, you can make your projects **faster, more organized, and more interactive**.

1. Using Functions with Parameters and Return Values

Functions can **take input parameters** and **return values**, allowing your program to process data efficiently.

Example: A Function That Doubles a Number

```
int doubleNumber(int num) {

  return num * 2;   // Multiply input by 2 and return
result

}


void setup() {

  Serial.begin(9600);

}


void loop() {

  int result = doubleNumber(5);   // Call function with 5

  Serial.println(result);   // Prints: 10

  delay(1000);

}
```

✓ What Happens?

- The function **doubleNumber()** takes a number, multiplies it by 2, and returns the result.

- The returned value is stored in result and printed in the **Serial Monitor**.

2. Using Function Pointers (More Flexible Code)

Function pointers allow you to **store functions inside variables**, making it easier to change program behavior dynamically.

Example: Using Function Pointers

```
void blinkFast() {

  digitalWrite(13, HIGH);
```

```
  delay(200);

  digitalWrite(13, LOW);

  delay(200);

}


void blinkSlow() {

  digitalWrite(13, HIGH);

  delay(1000);

  digitalWrite(13, LOW);

  delay(1000);

}


void (*blinkFunction)();  // Function pointer


void setup() {

  pinMode(13, OUTPUT);

  blinkFunction = blinkFast;  // Start with fast blinking

}


void loop() {

  blinkFunction();  // Call the function using pointer

}
```

✓ What Happens?

- The variable **blinkFunction** stores the function to be used.

- The **loop() calls blinkFunction()**, which executes blinkFast().

- You can later change **blinkFunction = blinkSlow;** to modify the behavior dynamically.

3. Using Interrupts for Fast Response

Interrupts allow your Arduino to **respond immediately** to an event, rather than waiting for the loop() to check.

Example: Using an Interrupt for a Button Press

```
int buttonPin = 2;

volatile bool buttonPressed = false;


void buttonISR() {

  buttonPressed = true;  // Set flag when button is
pressed

}


void setup() {

  Serial.begin(9600);

  pinMode(buttonPin, INPUT_PULLUP);

  attachInterrupt(digitalPinToInterrupt(buttonPin),
buttonISR, FALLING);

}


void loop() {

  if (buttonPressed) {

    Serial.println("Button Pressed!");

    buttonPressed = false;

  }

}
```

✓ What Happens?

- attachInterrupt() detects a **button press immediately**, rather than waiting in loop().

- The buttonISR() function sets buttonPressed = true, signaling the main loop.

4. Working with Timers (More Accurate Delays)

Using delay() stops your entire program. Instead, timers can run tasks **without blocking execution**.

Example: Blinking Without delay() Using millis()

```
const int ledPin = 13;

unsigned long previousTime = 0;

int interval = 1000;   // Blink every second


void setup() {

  pinMode(ledPin, OUTPUT);

}


void loop() {

  unsigned long currentTime = millis();


  if (currentTime - previousTime >= interval) {

    previousTime = currentTime;

    digitalWrite(ledPin, !digitalRead(ledPin));   // Toggle
LED

  }

}
```

✓ What Happens?

- The LED blinks **without stopping the program**.

- millis() tracks **elapsed time**, allowing other code to run.

5. Using PROGMEM to Save Memory

Arduino boards have **limited RAM**. **PROGMEM** stores constant data in **Flash memory** instead of RAM.

Example: Storing Text in PROGMEM

```
#include <avr/pgmspace.h>


const char message[] PROGMEM = "Hello from PROGMEM!";


void setup() {
  Serial.begin(9600);
  Serial.println((__FlashStringHelper*)message);
}


void loop() {}
```

✓ **What Happens?**

- The text "Hello from PROGMEM!" is stored in **Flash memory**, not RAM.

- Useful for **large text storage**, saving **precious RAM space**.

6. Summary: Why Use Advanced Functions?

✓ **Improve efficiency** – Functions **reduce repetition** and keep code organized.
✓ **Enhance flexibility** – **Function pointers and interrupts** allow dynamic control.
✓ **Enable real-time response** – **Interrupts and timers** improve performance.
✓ **Optimize memory usage** – **PROGMEM** prevents RAM overflow.

By mastering these advanced functions, you can build **faster, more efficient, and smarter Arduino projects**!

Enhancing projects with additional capabilities

As you advance in Arduino programming, you can **expand your projects by adding more powerful features**. By using **external libraries, advanced functions, and communication protocols**, you can create **more interactive and complex systems**.

1. Adding Wireless Communication (WiFi & Bluetooth)

Modern projects often require **wireless control and data transmission**. You can add **WiFi or Bluetooth** modules to make your projects **remote-controllable and internet-connected**.

Example: Connecting Arduino to WiFi (ESP8266 or ESP32)

The **ESP8266 WiFi module** allows Arduino to **connect to the internet** and send data.

Code: Connecting to WiFi

```
#include <ESP8266WiFi.h>


const char* ssid = "YourNetwork";
const char* password = "YourPassword";


void setup() {
  Serial.begin(115200);
  WiFi.begin(ssid, password);


  while (WiFi.status() != WL_CONNECTED) {
    delay(1000);
    Serial.println("Connecting...");
  }
```

```
  Serial.println("Connected!");
}


void loop() {
}
```

✓ The Arduino connects to **WiFi**, enabling **IoT projects** like **remote monitoring and control**.

2. Displaying Data on OLED or TFT Screens

Instead of using just the **Serial Monitor**, you can display data on **OLED or TFT screens** for a more interactive experience.

Example: Displaying Text on an OLED Screen

Using the **Adafruit SSD1306 library**, you can **show sensor readings on an OLED display**.

Code: Displaying "Hello, Arduino!" on OLED

```
#include <Wire.h>

#include <Adafruit_GFX.h>

#include <Adafruit_SSD1306.h>


Adafruit_SSD1306 display(128, 64, &Wire, -1);


void setup() {
  display.begin(SSD1306_SWITCHCAPVCC, 0x3C);

  display.clearDisplay();

  display.setTextSize(1);

  display.setTextColor(WHITE);

  display.setCursor(0, 10);

  display.print("Hello, Arduino!");
```

```
  display.display();

}
```

```
void loop() {

}
```

✓ The OLED screen **displays text and graphics**, making projects more user-friendly.

3. Controlling Projects with a Smartphone (Bluetooth)

Using the **HC-05 Bluetooth module**, you can **control Arduino projects wirelessly** using a smartphone.

Example: Controlling an LED via Bluetooth

Wiring:

- **HC-05 TX → Arduino RX (Pin 10)**

- **HC-05 RX → Arduino TX (Pin 11)**

Code: Receiving Bluetooth Commands

```
#include <SoftwareSerial.h>


SoftwareSerial BT(10, 11);   // TX, RX


int ledPin = 13;


void setup() {
  pinMode(ledPin, OUTPUT);
  BT.begin(9600);
}
```

```
void loop() {
  if (BT.available()) {
    char command = BT.read();
    if (command == '1') {
      digitalWrite(ledPin, HIGH);
    } else if (command == '0') {
      digitalWrite(ledPin, LOW);
    }
  }
}
```

✓ The **LED turns ON/OFF** based on Bluetooth commands sent from a smartphone.

4. Using Sensors for Smart Applications

Sensors allow your Arduino to **interact with the real world**. You can use:
✓ **Motion sensors** → Trigger alarms or automatic lights.
✓ **Temperature & humidity sensors** → Build a smart weather station.
✓ **Light sensors** → Adjust brightness based on ambient light.

Example: Automatic Light Control with an LDR (Light Sensor)

```
int ldrPin = A0;

int ledPin = 9;


void setup() {
  pinMode(ledPin, OUTPUT);
  Serial.begin(9600);
}


void loop() {
```

```
  int lightLevel = analogRead(ldrPin);
  if (lightLevel < 500) {
    digitalWrite(ledPin, HIGH);
  } else {
    digitalWrite(ledPin, LOW);
  }
}
```

✓ The **LED turns ON in darkness and OFF in bright light** automatically.

5. Storing and Logging Data (SD Card)

You can **log sensor data to an SD card** for later analysis.

Example: Writing Data to an SD Card

```
#include <SD.h>

const int chipSelect = 10;
int sensorPin = A0;

void setup() {
  Serial.begin(9600);
  SD.begin(chipSelect);
}

void loop() {
  File dataFile = SD.open("log.txt", FILE_WRITE);
  if (dataFile) {
    int sensorValue = analogRead(sensorPin);
    dataFile.println(sensorValue);
```

```
    dataFile.close();
  }
  delay(1000);
}
```

✓ **Data is saved to an SD card**, useful for **data logging applications**.

6. Summary: Expanding Your Arduino Projects

✓ **Wireless Control** – Use **WiFi & Bluetooth** for **remote monitoring**.
✓ **Better Displays** – Show data on **OLED/TFT screens** instead of just Serial Monitor.
✓ **Smart Sensors** – Automate lights, security, and weather systems.
✓ **Data Logging** – Store readings on **SD cards for later analysis**.

By incorporating these **advanced features**, you can **turn basic Arduino projects into fully functional smart systems**!

Project: Building a Simple Application

Designing a project from scratch

Before you start writing code, it's important to **plan your project properly**. Good design ensures that your project is **efficient, well-structured, and easy to troubleshoot**.

1. Define the Project Goal

Start by answering:

✓ **What will your project do?** (e.g., Control LEDs, measure temperature, send data to a phone)

✓ **What components will you need?** (e.g., Sensors, displays, buttons, WiFi modules)

✓ **How will the user interact with it?** (e.g., Button press, touchscreen, voice command)

Example: Smart Temperature Monitoring System

✅ **Goal:** Measure room temperature and display it on an **OLED screen**.

✅ **User Interaction:** The user can press a button to switch between °C and °F.

✅ **Components:**

- **DHT11 sensor** (to measure temperature)

- **OLED display** (to show data)

- **Push button** (to toggle °C/°F)

- **Arduino Nano** (to process everything)

2. Select the Right Components

Once the goal is clear, make a **list of required components** and check their compatibility.

Component	Function
DHT11	Reads temperature and humidity
OLED Display (SSD1306)	Displays temperature readings
Push Button	Switches between Celsius and Fahrenheit
Arduino Nano	Controls the entire system

◆ **Tip:** Check datasheets to ensure components operate at the same voltage (e.g., 5V for Arduino Nano).

3. Plan the Circuit Connections

Before coding, create a **circuit diagram** to understand how components will connect.

Component	Arduino Pin
DHT11	D2
OLED Display (I2C)	SDA → A4, SCL → A5
Push Button	D3

Example: Wiring for Smart Temperature Monitor

- **DHT11 sensor** → Connects to **D2**

- **OLED Display (I2C) → SDA → A4, SCL → A5**

- **Push Button → D3**

4. Break the Project into Small Tasks

Instead of writing everything at once, divide the project into **smaller, manageable parts**:

✅ **Step 1:** Test the **DHT11 sensor** (print temperature to Serial Monitor).
✅ **Step 2:** Display temperature on the **OLED screen**.
✅ **Step 3:** Program the **button** to switch °C/°F.
✅ **Step 4:** Combine all parts into a **final working program**.

5. Write a Simple Flowchart or Pseudocode

A flowchart helps **visualize the logic** of your program.

Flowchart for Smart Temperature Monitor:
1️⃣Start
2️⃣Read **temperature from DHT11**
3️⃣If the button is pressed, **toggle between °C and °F**
4️⃣Display temperature on **OLED screen**
5️⃣Repeat

Pseudocode:

```
Start

Initialize DHT11 and OLED

Loop:

    Read temperature from DHT11

    If button pressed:

        Toggle between Celsius/Fahrenheit

    Display temperature on OLED

Repeat
```

✓ This makes coding **easier and more structured**.

6. Prepare for Coding

Before you start coding:
✓ Install necessary **Arduino libraries** (e.g., DHT.h for sensors, Adafruit_SSD1306.h for OLED).
✓ Verify **sensor connections** by running test code.
✓ Keep code **modular** using **functions** (e.g., readTemperature(), displayData()).

Summary: How to Design a Project from Scratch

✓ **Define the project goal** – What will it do? How will users interact with it?
✓ **Select the right components** – Choose compatible parts.
✓ **Plan circuit connections** – Know which pins to use.
✓ **Break into smaller tasks** – Test components step by step.
✓ **Write a flowchart or pseudocode** – Plan the logic before coding.

By following these steps, you can **design Arduino projects efficiently** and avoid unnecessary troubleshooting later!

Implementing the code

Once you have designed your project, the next step is to **write the code and bring your idea to life**. Good implementation ensures that your program is **organized, efficient, and easy to modify**.

1. Set Up the Arduino IDE

Before you start coding, make sure:

✓ You have the **Arduino IDE installed**.

✓ All **required libraries** are installed.

✓ Your **Arduino Nano is connected** and recognized by the IDE.

Example: Smart Temperature Monitoring System

We will now write the code for a **temperature display system** using:

✓ **DHT11 sensor** (to measure temperature)

✓ **OLED display** (to show readings)

✓ **Push button** (to switch between °C and °F)

2. Include Necessary Libraries

Before writing any logic, include the required libraries.

```
#include <Wire.h>

#include <Adafruit_GFX.h>

#include <Adafruit_SSD1306.h>

#include <DHT.h>
```

✓ The Adafruit_SSD1306.h library helps control the **OLED screen**.

✓ The DHT.h library reads **temperature from the DHT11 sensor**.

3. Define Pins and Variables

Next, define which pins the **sensor, button, and display** are connected to.

```
#define DHTPIN 2          // DHT11 sensor on pin 2

#define BUTTONPIN 3       // Push button on pin 3

#define DHTTYPE DHT11     // Define sensor type
```

```
DHT dht(DHTPIN, DHTTYPE);

Adafruit_SSD1306 display(128, 64, &Wire, -1);


bool isCelsius = true;   // Variable to track unit
selection
```

✓ The **DHT sensor** is connected to pin **D2**.
✓ The **button is on D3** and will switch between **Celsius and Fahrenheit**.

4. Initialize Components in setup()

In setup(), initialize the **sensor, button, and display**.

```
void setup() {

  pinMode(BUTTONPIN, INPUT_PULLUP);   // Use internal pull-
up resistor

  dht.begin();


  display.begin(SSD1306_SWITCHCAPVCC, 0x3C);

  display.clearDisplay();

  display.setTextSize(1);

  display.setTextColor(WHITE);

}
```

✓ The **button uses INPUT_PULLUP** to avoid external resistors.
✓ The **display is set up** with a resolution of 128x64.

5. Read Temperature and Display Data

Inside loop(), read temperature from the **DHT11 sensor** and display it.

```
void loop() {

  float tempC = dht.readTemperature();   // Read
temperature in Celsius
```

```
  float tempF = tempC * 9 / 5 + 32;     // Convert to
Fahrenheit


  if (digitalRead(BUTTONPIN) == LOW) {  // Check if button
is pressed

    isCelsius = !isCelsius;  // Toggle between Celsius and
Fahrenheit

    delay(300);  // Debounce delay

  }


  display.clearDisplay();

  display.setCursor(0, 10);

  display.print("Temp: ");

  display.print(isCelsius ? tempC : tempF); // Show temp
in selected unit

  display.print(isCelsius ? " C" : " F");

  display.display();


  delay(1000);

}
```

✓ The **temperature is read** and converted to **Fahrenheit**.
✓ The **button toggles between Celsius and Fahrenheit**.
✓ The **OLED display updates** with the correct unit.

6. Test the Code on Your Arduino Nano

✓ **Compile and upload the code** to your Arduino Nano.
✓ **Check the Serial Monitor** for any errors or missing data.
✓ **Press the button** to confirm that the unit toggles between **°C and °F**.

Summary: Steps to Implement the Code

✓ **Include required libraries** to control sensors and displays.

✓ **Define pin connections** for all components.

✓ **Initialize devices in setup()** to prepare for execution.

✓ **Write logic in loop()** to read sensors, process data, and display output.

✓ **Upload and test** the code to verify everything works.

With the code implemented, the next step is **testing and troubleshooting** to ensure smooth operation!

Testing and troubleshooting

After writing and uploading your code, the next step is to **test your project and fix any issues**. Troubleshooting is an important skill that helps you identify and correct **errors in wiring, code, or logic**.

1. Start with Basic Checks

Before deep troubleshooting, check for **common mistakes**:

✓ **Power Supply** – Is the Arduino properly powered?

✓ **Connections** – Are all wires and components connected correctly?

✓ **Correct Port & Board** – In Arduino IDE, go to **Tools → Port** and select the right board.

✓ **Library Installation** – Have you installed all required libraries?

2. Use the Serial Monitor for Debugging

The **Serial Monitor** is a great tool for finding **errors in your program**. You can use it to **print sensor readings, check button presses, or debug logic issues**.

Example: Checking Sensor Data in Serial Monitor

```
void setup() {

  Serial.begin(9600);  // Start Serial Monitor

}


void loop() {

  int sensorValue = analogRead(A0);  // Read sensor value

  Serial.print("Sensor Value: ");
```

```
    Serial.println(sensorValue);   // Print to Serial Monitor

    delay(500);

}
```

✓ If the **Serial Monitor shows wrong or no values**, check wiring or sensor connections.

3. Testing Each Component Separately

If your project has **multiple components**, test each one **individually** before combining them.

✓ **Step 1:** Test the **sensor alone** – Does it return expected values?
✓ **Step 2:** Test the **display separately** – Does it show any text?
✓ **Step 3:** Test the **button function** – Does pressing the button change anything?

Example: Testing a Button Before Using It in a Larger Program

```
void setup() {

  pinMode(3, INPUT_PULLUP);

  Serial.begin(9600);

}


void loop() {

  if (digitalRead(3) == LOW) {

    Serial.println("Button Pressed!");

    delay(300);   // Debounce delay

  }

}
```

✓ If **"Button Pressed!"** doesn't appear, check the **wiring or button orientation**.

4. Common Problems and Solutions

(A) Code Compiles But Doesn't Work?

◆ Possible Issues & Fixes:

✓ Check if the correct **board and port** are selected in **Tools → Board** and **Tools → Port**.

✓ Use Serial.println() to check if your **code is running at all**.

(B) Sensor Returns 0 or NaN?

◆ Possible Issues & Fixes:

✓ Verify sensor **wiring (VCC, GND, Signal)**.

✓ Add a short **delay** (delay(500);) before reading data.

(C) LED Doesn't Light Up?

◆ Possible Issues & Fixes:

✓ Try **replacing the LED**.

✓ Make sure you have a **resistor (220Ω–1kΩ)** in series with the LED.

✓ Test with digitalWrite(13, HIGH); to force the LED ON.

5. Testing the Complete Project

Once individual components work, test the **entire project** step by step:

✅ **Run the program and observe outputs**.

✅ **Check for unexpected behavior** (e.g., incorrect temperature display).

✅ **Ensure smooth interaction** (button presses change display, readings update).

✅ **Make small changes and test again**.

6. Final Debugging Checklist

✓ **Power and connections are correct**.

✓ **Code compiles without errors**.

✓ **Serial Monitor shows expected values**.

✓ **Components work individually and together**.

✓ **No unexpected resets or malfunctions**.

Summary: How to Test and Troubleshoot Your Project

✓ **Check wiring and power connections** first.

✓ **Use Serial Monitor** to debug and print sensor values.

✓ **Test components separately** before combining them.

✓ **Fix common issues** like incorrect ports, faulty sensors, or missing resistors.

✓ **Run the full project, observe behavior, and refine the code**.

By following these steps, you can **quickly identify and fix issues**, making your Arduino project work smoothly!

Troubleshooting and Best Practices

Common issues and solutions

When working with Arduino, you might encounter problems with **code errors, hardware issues, or unexpected behavior**. Below are some of the **most common issues** and **simple solutions** to fix them quickly.

1. Code Compiles but Doesn't Work

✦ **Problem:** The code uploads successfully, but nothing happens.

✅ **Solutions:**
✓ Check that the **correct board and port** are selected in **Tools → Board** and **Tools → Port**.
✓ Use Serial.println("Test"); to check if the **code is running**.
✓ Ensure you have a setup() and loop() function in your code.

2. Arduino Not Recognized by Computer

✦ **Problem:** The Arduino Nano does not show up in the **Arduino IDE**.

✅ **Solutions:**
✓ Try using a **different USB cable** (some cables only provide power, not data).
✓ Go to **Tools → Port** and select the right COM port.
✓ If using a **clone Arduino Nano**, install the **CH340 driver** for USB communication.

3. LED or Motor Not Working

✦ **Problem:** The LED, motor, or other output device is not responding.

✅ **Solutions:**
✓ If using an **LED**, check if it is **connected in the right direction** (long leg = positive).
✓ Try using **digitalWrite(LED_PIN, HIGH);** to manually turn the LED on.
✓ If using a **motor**, ensure it has **enough power** (some motors need an external power source).

4. Sensor Always Returns 0, NaN, or Incorrect Values

◆ **Problem:** Sensor readings do not change or return **zero or NaN (Not a Number)**.

✅ **Solutions:**
✓ Double-check **wiring (VCC, GND, Signal)**.
✓ Add a **short delay (delay(500);)** before reading sensor data.
✓ If using an analog sensor, verify you are using the correct **analog pin (A0-A5)**.

5. Button Presses Not Registering

◆ **Problem:** Pressing a button does not trigger the expected response.

✅ **Solutions:**
✓ If using INPUT, add an **external pull-down resistor (10kΩ to GND)**.
✓ Use INPUT_PULLUP instead of INPUT to enable an **internal pull-up resistor**.
✓ Add a **debounce delay** to prevent multiple detections from one press:

```
if (digitalRead(buttonPin) == LOW) {

  delay(50);  // Debounce

  if (digitalRead(buttonPin) == LOW) {

    Serial.println("Button Pressed!");

  }

}
```

6. Unexpected Resets or Freezing

◆ **Problem:** The Arduino **randomly restarts or stops responding**.

✅ **Solutions:**
✓ If using motors or relays, ensure the power supply **provides enough current**.
✓ Avoid using delay() for long pauses—use millis() instead.
✓ Check for **infinite loops (while(true))** that may block execution.

7. Code Too Slow or Unresponsive

◆ **Problem:** The program runs **slowly** or **doesn't respond quickly to inputs**.

✅ **Solutions:**
✓ **Replace delay() with millis()** to keep the program responsive.
✓ Optimize loops by **reducing unnecessary calculations** inside loop().

✓ Use **interrupts** for real-time response instead of constantly checking input in loop().

Summary: Quick Troubleshooting Checklist

✓ **Check connections and power supply.**

✓ **Use Serial Monitor to debug (Serial.println()).**

✓ **Test components separately** before combining them.

✓ **Use INPUT_PULLUP for buttons to avoid floating pins.**

✓ **Replace delay() with millis()** for better performance.

By following these simple solutions, you can **quickly identify and fix issues**, ensuring your Arduino projects work smoothly!

Optimizing your code

Writing optimized code makes your Arduino project **faster, more efficient, and easier to maintain**. Optimized code reduces memory usage, avoids delays, and ensures smooth performance, especially for **real-time applications** like robotics and sensor data processing.

1. Avoid Using delay(), Use millis() Instead

The delay() function **pauses everything**, preventing the Arduino from doing other tasks. Instead, use millis() to track elapsed time without stopping execution.

Example: Blinking an LED Without delay()

```
const int ledPin = 13;

unsigned long previousMillis = 0;

int interval = 1000;   // 1-second blink interval


void setup() {

  pinMode(ledPin, OUTPUT);

}


void loop() {
```

```
unsigned long currentMillis = millis();


if (currentMillis - previousMillis >= interval) {

    previousMillis = currentMillis;

    digitalWrite(ledPin, !digitalRead(ledPin));  // Toggle
LED

  }

}
```

✓ The LED blinks **without pausing the program**, allowing other tasks to run simultaneously.

2. Use Arrays Instead of Multiple Variables

Instead of defining multiple variables for **similar data**, use an **array** and a loop to process values efficiently.

Example: Controlling Multiple LEDs with an Array

```
int ledPins[] = {3, 5, 6, 9, 10, 11};  // LED pins


void setup() {

  for (int i = 0; i < 6; i++) {

    pinMode(ledPins[i], OUTPUT);

  }

}


void loop() {

  for (int i = 0; i < 6; i++) {

    digitalWrite(ledPins[i], HIGH);

    delay(200);

    digitalWrite(ledPins[i], LOW);
```

```
  }
}
```

✓ This reduces **code repetition** and makes it easier to **add or remove LEDs** later.

3. Use Functions to Avoid Repetition

Functions **organize your code**, making it reusable and easier to modify.

Example: Creating a Function for Blinking

```
void blinkLED(int pin, int time) {

  digitalWrite(pin, HIGH);

  delay(time);

  digitalWrite(pin, LOW);

  delay(time);

}


void setup() {

  pinMode(13, OUTPUT);

}


void loop() {

  blinkLED(13, 500);   // Blink LED with a 500ms delay

}
```

✓ If you need to change the **blink speed or add more LEDs**, you only update the **function**, not every part of the code.

4. Use const and #define for Fixed Values

Using const or #define improves efficiency and prevents accidental changes.

Example: Using const and #define

```
const int ledPin = 13;   // LED pin (constant)
```

```
#define DELAY_TIME 500     // Delay time (macro)

void setup() {
  pinMode(ledPin, OUTPUT);
}

void loop() {
  digitalWrite(ledPin, HIGH);
  delay(DELAY_TIME);
  digitalWrite(ledPin, LOW);
  delay(DELAY_TIME);
}
```

✓ **Constants use less memory** and **improve readability**.

5. Minimize Memory Usage with PROGMEM

Arduino has limited RAM. Use **PROGMEM** to store large arrays or text in Flash memory instead of RAM.

Example: Storing Messages in PROGMEM

```
#include <avr/pgmspace.h>

const char message[] PROGMEM = "Hello from PROGMEM!";

void setup() {
  Serial.begin(9600);
  Serial.println((__FlashStringHelper*)message);
}
```

```
void loop() {}
```

✓ This **saves RAM space** by storing text in Flash memory.

6. Use Efficient Data Types

Use the **smallest data type** needed to reduce memory usage.

- ◆ **Use byte or uint8_t** instead of int for values between **0 and 255**.
- ◆ **Use bool** instead of int for **true/false values**.

Example: Using Smaller Data Types

```
byte sensorValue = 255;  // Takes 1 byte (vs. 2 bytes for
int)

bool isOn = true;        // Takes 1 byte (vs. 2 bytes for
int)
```

✓ This saves memory, especially in **memory-limited boards** like Arduino Nano.

7. Avoid Unnecessary Global Variables

Global variables take up memory even when **not in use**. If a variable is only needed inside a function, define it **inside the function** instead of making it global.

Example: Using Local Variables Instead of Global

```
void loop() {

   int sensorValue = analogRead(A0);  // Local variable
(better memory usage)

   Serial.println(sensorValue);

   delay(1000);

}
```

✓ The variable **sensorValue only exists inside loop()**, freeing memory when not in use.

Summary: How to Optimize Your Arduino Code

✓ **Replace delay() with millis()** for better performance.
✓ **Use arrays and loops** instead of multiple variables.
✓ **Create functions** to reuse code efficiently.

✓ **Use const and PROGMEM** to save memory.

✓ **Choose efficient data types** (use byte instead of int when possible).

✓ **Avoid unnecessary global variables** to free up RAM.

By following these **optimization techniques**, your Arduino projects will be **faster, more memory-efficient, and easier to manage**!

Tips for effective debugging

Debugging is an essential skill in Arduino programming. It helps you **find and fix errors quickly**, ensuring your project runs smoothly. Here are some simple yet effective techniques to debug your Arduino code.

1. Use the Serial Monitor for Debugging

The **Serial Monitor** is your best tool for checking if your code is working correctly. You can use it to **print sensor values, confirm button presses, and track program flow**.

Example: Checking Sensor Readings in Serial Monitor

```
void setup() {

  Serial.begin(9600);  // Start Serial Monitor

}


void loop() {

  int sensorValue = analogRead(A0);

  Serial.print("Sensor Value: ");

  Serial.println(sensorValue);  // Print to Serial Monitor

  delay(500);

}
```

✓ If the **Serial Monitor shows no values**, check **wiring or sensor connections**.

✓ If values are **unexpected**, there might be a **coding error or faulty sensor**.

2. Add Debugging Messages to Track Code Execution

If your code isn't running as expected, use Serial.println() to check **which parts are executing**.

Example: Checking Button Press Detection

```
void setup() {

  Serial.begin(9600);

  pinMode(3, INPUT_PULLUP);

}


void loop() {

  if (digitalRead(3) == LOW) {

    Serial.println("Button Pressed!");  // Confirms button
is detected

    delay(300);  // Debounce delay

  }

}
```

✓ If **"Button Pressed!"** doesn't appear in the Serial Monitor, **check wiring or the button**.

3. Test Components One by One

If your project has **multiple components (sensors, motors, displays)**, test **each part separately** before combining them.

◆ **Step 1:** Test the **sensor** alone.
◆ **Step 2:** Test the **display** separately.
◆ **Step 3:** Test the **button press function**.
◆ **Step 4:** Combine all parts after individual testing.

4. Check for Infinite Loops or Blocking Code

If your Arduino **stops responding**, it may be stuck in an **infinite loop** or waiting too long in delay().

Example: A Loop That Freezes Execution

```
void loop() {

  while (true) {  // Infinite loop
```

```
    Serial.println("Stuck here!");

    delay(1000);

  }

}
```

✅ **Fix:** Instead of an infinite loop, use conditions to **exit the loop when needed**.

5. Replace delay() with millis() for Better Debugging

Using delay() **stops all other functions**, making debugging harder. Instead, use millis() for non-blocking timing.

Example: Debugging with millis() Instead of delay()

```
unsigned long previousMillis = 0;

const int interval = 1000;


void setup() {

  Serial.begin(9600);

}


void loop() {

  unsigned long currentMillis = millis();

  if (currentMillis - previousMillis >= interval) {

    previousMillis = currentMillis;

    Serial.println("1 second passed");

  }

}
```

✓ The program **continues running while printing messages every second**.

6. Double-Check Power and Wiring Connections

◆ **Common Wiring Mistakes:**
✓ Wrong **pin connections** (check component datasheets).
✓ **Loose wires** (especially with breadboards).
✓ Insufficient **power supply** (some motors and displays need external power).

7. Use F() Macro to Save Memory When Printing Strings

If you print a lot of text to the Serial Monitor, it uses valuable **RAM**. Use F() to store strings in **Flash memory instead of RAM**.

Example: Saving RAM with F()

```
Serial.println(F("This string is stored in Flash, not
RAM!"));
```

✓ This helps prevent **out-of-memory errors** on small Arduino boards like the Nano.

8. Use #define and const for Readability

Instead of **hardcoding values**, use **constants** to make your code clearer and easier to modify.

Example: Using Constants for Readability

```
#define LED_PIN 13

const int BUTTON_PIN = 3;


void setup() {

  pinMode(LED_PIN, OUTPUT);

  pinMode(BUTTON_PIN, INPUT_PULLUP);

}
```

✓ This makes it **easier to update pin numbers** later if needed.

9. Reset the Arduino if Unexpected Errors Occur

If your Arduino behaves **erratically**, try resetting it:
✓ **Press the reset button** on the board.
✓ **Disconnect and reconnect** the USB cable.
✓ **Upload a blank sketch** (setup() and loop() with nothing inside) to clear memory.

10. Read Error Messages in the Arduino IDE

If your code doesn't compile, check the **error messages at the bottom of the Arduino IDE**.

◈ **Common Errors & Fixes:**

Error Message	Possible Cause	Solution
expected ';' before	Missing semicolon ;	Add ; at the end of the line
not declared in this scope	Variable not defined	Check spelling or define the variable before using it
redefinition of 'void setup()'	Duplicated setup() or loop()	Ensure setup() and loop() appear **only once**
board not found	Wrong USB port or bad cable	Check **Tools → Port** and use a **different USB cable**

Summary: Effective Debugging Tips

✓ **Use Serial Monitor (Serial.println())** to check sensor values and track program execution.

✓ **Test components separately** before combining them.

✓ **Check for infinite loops or long delays (delay()) that block execution.**

✓ **Replace delay() with millis()** for better performance.

✓ **Verify power and wiring connections** if components don't work.

✓ **Use F() macro to save RAM when printing text.**

✓ **Read error messages carefully** to find issues quickly.

By following these **debugging techniques**, you can **quickly identify and fix issues**, making your Arduino projects work reliably!

Next Steps and Further Resources

Exploring more complex projects

Now that you understand the basics of Arduino programming, it's time to **take your skills to the next level** by working on **more advanced projects**. These projects involve **multiple components**, require **more efficient coding**, and introduce **new technologies** such as wireless communication, IoT, and automation.

1. Expanding Your Knowledge with Advanced Projects

Here are some **challenging project ideas** that will help you apply and enhance your Arduino skills:

Project	Key Features	Components Used
Smart Weather Station	Displays real-time temperature, humidity, and pressure	DHT11/DHT22, BMP180, OLED screen, SD card
Home Automation System	Controls lights and appliances remotely via smartphone	Relay module, Bluetooth/WiFi, Mobile app
Obstacle-Avoiding Robot	Moves autonomously and avoids obstacles	Ultrasonic sensor, Motors, Servo, Motor driver
IoT Temperature Monitor	Sends temperature data to an online dashboard	ESP8266/ESP32, DHT11, Cloud service (Thingspeak)
Fingerprint Door Lock	Unlocks a door using a fingerprint scanner	Fingerprint sensor, Servo, Keypad

2. Combining Multiple Technologies

As you move to complex projects, you'll need to **combine multiple technologies**:

✓ **Wireless Communication** → Use **WiFi (ESP8266, ESP32)** or **Bluetooth (HC-05, BLE)** for remote control.

✓ **Data Logging** → Store sensor data on an **SD card** for future analysis.
✓ **Cloud Integration** → Send data to the internet using **MQTT, Blynk, or Thingspeak**.
✓ **Mobile App Control** → Use **MIT App Inventor** or **Blynk** to control projects from your smartphone.

3. Example: IoT Smart Home System

Features:

✓ **Remotely control lights and fans** using a smartphone.
✓ **Monitor temperature and humidity** in real-time.
✓ **Receive alerts** if temperature exceeds a certain limit.

Required Components:

- **ESP8266/ESP32** (WiFi module)

- **Relay module** (to control appliances)

- **DHT11/DHT22** (temperature and humidity sensor)

- **Blynk App** (for smartphone control)

Basic Code Structure:

```
#include <ESP8266WiFi.h>

#include <BlynkSimpleEsp8266.h>

#include <DHT.h>


#define DHTPIN D2

#define RELAY_PIN D1

DHT dht(DHTPIN, DHT11);


char auth[] = "YourBlynkAuthToken";

char ssid[] = "YourWiFiSSID";

char pass[] = "YourWiFiPassword";
```

```
void setup() {

  Serial.begin(115200);

  Blynk.begin(auth, ssid, pass);

  pinMode(RELAY_PIN, OUTPUT);

  dht.begin();

}


void loop() {

  float temp = dht.readTemperature();

  Blynk.virtualWrite(V1, temp);

  if (temp > 30) {

    digitalWrite(RELAY_PIN, HIGH);  // Turn on fan if temp
> 30°C

  }

  Blynk.run();

}
```

✓ The ESP8266 **connects to WiFi**, sends **temperature data to Blynk**, and **turns on a fan** if the temperature exceeds 30°C.

4. Improving Code Efficiency and Modularity

As your projects grow in complexity, **modular programming** becomes essential.

✓ **Use separate functions** for different tasks (readTemperature(), controlRelay()).
✓ **Use object-oriented programming (OOP)** when working with multiple sensors or devices.
✓ **Store large data in PROGMEM** to save RAM when working with text-based outputs.

5. Summary: How to Approach Complex Projects

✓ **Choose a challenging project** that incorporates new technologies.
✓ **Learn about wireless communication, IoT, and automation.**

✓ **Work with cloud services and mobile apps** for remote monitoring.
✓ **Organize code using modular programming** for efficiency.
✓ **Use best practices like millis() for non-blocking execution**.

By exploring these advanced projects, you will **enhance your Arduino skills** and be ready to build **real-world applications!**

Continuing your learning journey

Now that you've mastered the basics of **Arduino programming**, it's time to **keep learning and improving your skills**. The world of electronics and embedded systems is vast, and there are **endless possibilities** for creative projects. Here's how you can **keep growing as an Arduino developer**.

1. Expand Your Knowledge with New Topics

To go beyond basic Arduino projects, explore **more advanced concepts**:

Topic	Why It's Useful
Internet of Things (IoT)	Connect your projects to the internet (WiFi, MQTT, Blynk).
Wireless Communication	Use **Bluetooth, LoRa, or RFID** for remote control.
Automation & Robotics	Build **self-driving robots, AI-based systems, and home automation**.
Machine Learning on Microcontrollers	Use **TinyML** to add AI features to Arduino projects.
Embedded Systems Programming	Learn **C++ OOP for Arduino** and **low-level microcontroller programming**.

2. Work on Real-World Projects

The best way to **improve your skills** is by working on **real-world projects**. Here are some ideas:

✅ **Smart Agriculture System** – Monitor **soil moisture and temperature**, then control irrigation automatically.
✅ **Voice-Controlled Home Automation** – Control appliances using **voice**

commands with a **Google Assistant** or **Alexa**.

✓ **AI-Powered Face Recognition System** – Use **ESP32-CAM** to recognize faces and unlock doors.

✓ **Weather Station with Web Dashboard** – Send temperature and humidity data to a **web dashboard** for remote monitoring.

◆ **Tip:** Document your projects on **GitHub, blogs, or social media** to share your progress with the community.

3. Learn New Programming Techniques

As you develop more advanced projects, you'll need to **improve your coding techniques**:

✓ **Use Object-Oriented Programming (OOP)** – Make reusable libraries for sensors and devices.

✓ **Optimize memory usage** – Use PROGMEM to store large strings and images in Flash memory.

✓ **Reduce power consumption** – Learn **sleep modes and energy-saving techniques** for battery-powered projects.

✓ **Use FreeRTOS** – Run **multiple tasks at once** on ESP32 or ARM-based microcontrollers.

4. Experiment with Different Microcontrollers

While **Arduino Uno and Nano** are great for beginners, consider learning about **more powerful microcontrollers**:

Microcontroller	Features
ESP32	Built-in WiFi & Bluetooth, faster CPU, dual-core.
Raspberry Pi Pico	Runs **MicroPython** and C++, has better performance.
STM32	Used in **industrial automation and robotics**.
Teensy 4.1	High-speed processing for **audio and real-time applications**.

5. Participate in Hackathons and Open-Source Projects

◆ **Join online competitions** – Platforms like **Hackster.io** and **Arduino Project Hub** host **challenges** where you can win prizes.

◆ **Contribute to open-source projects** – Improve existing **Arduino libraries** or create your own.

◆ **Collaborate with the maker community** – Join **GitHub, forums, and Discord groups** to learn from others.

6. Summary: How to Keep Learning Arduino

✓ **Explore advanced topics** – IoT, robotics, AI, and embedded systems.

✓ **Work on real-world projects** – Apply what you've learned to practical applications.

✓ **Improve your coding skills** – Learn OOP, FreeRTOS, and power-saving techniques.

✓ **Try new microcontrollers** – Experiment with ESP32, STM32, and Raspberry Pi Pico.

✓ **Engage with the Arduino community** – Join forums, contribute to open-source projects, and participate in competitions.

By following these steps, you'll **continue growing as a skilled Arduino developer** and unlock new creative possibilities!

Recommended resources and communities

To continue learning and improving your Arduino skills, it's important to use **high-quality resources** and **engage with the Arduino community**. Here are some of the best places to find tutorials, ask questions, and collaborate with other makers.

1. Official Arduino Resources

✓ Arduino Website – Official guides, reference materials, and project ideas.
✓ **Arduino Forum** – Ask questions, get help, and discuss projects.
✓ **Arduino Project Hub** – Explore thousands of Arduino projects with step-by-step instructions.

2. Best Websites for Learning Arduino

✓ **SparkFun Tutorials** – Beginner to advanced electronics tutorials.
✓ **Adafruit Learning System** – Great for working with sensors, displays, and IoT devices.
✓ Instructables – Step-by-step guides on creative Arduino projects.
✓ Hackster.io – A platform where makers share innovative projects.

3. YouTube Channels for Arduino Learning

📹 Great video tutorials and project ideas:
✓ Paul McWhorter – Beginner-friendly Arduino programming.
✓ DroneBot Workshop – Deep dives into electronics and robotics.
✓ GreatScott! – Advanced Arduino and DIY electronics.
✓ Raspberry Pi & Arduino Tutorials – Covers both Arduino and Raspberry Pi.

4. Best Books for Learning Arduino

📚 Recommended Books for Beginners and Advanced Users:
✓ **"Arduino Cookbook" – Michael Margolis** – Covers Arduino basics to advanced techniques.
✓ **"Programming Arduino: Getting Started with Sketches" – Simon Monk** – A beginner-friendly guide.
✓ **"Exploring Arduino" – Jeremy Blum** – Deep dives into real-world projects.
✓ **"Arduino Robotics" – John-David Warren** – Learn how to build robots using Arduino.

5. Online Courses for Deeper Learning

📑 If you prefer structured learning, try these online courses:
✓ Udemy - Arduino Step by Step – Comprehensive Arduino courses.
✓ Coursera - Introduction to Embedded Systems – Learn embedded programming.
✓ edX - Internet of Things (IoT) with Arduino – Learn how to create IoT projects.

6. Join the Maker Community

Being part of a community helps you **learn faster, get support, and stay motivated**.

☐ Popular Arduino Communities:
✓ **Reddit: r/arduino** (https://www.reddit.com/r/arduino/) – Ask questions, share projects, and discuss Arduino.
✓ **Discord Groups** – Search for Arduino or IoT-related servers for live discussions.
✓ **Hackaday.io** (https://hackaday.io/) – A platform for inventors and DIY enthusiasts.

Summary: Where to Learn and Connect with Arduino Enthusiasts

✓ **Use the official Arduino website** for reference materials and guides.
✓ **Follow online tutorials** from sites like SparkFun, Adafruit, and Hackster.io.

✓ **Watch YouTube videos** from experts like DroneBot Workshop and Paul McWhorter.

✓ **Read books** to deepen your understanding of Arduino and electronics.

✓ **Take online courses** for structured learning.

✓ **Join communities on Reddit, Discord, and Hackaday.io** to get help and share your progress.

By using these resources and engaging with the Arduino community, you'll continue **growing your skills, finding inspiration, and building amazing projects**!

www.ingramcontent.com/pod-product-compliance
Lightning Source LLC
LaVergne TN
LVHW022351060326
832902LV00022B/4371